Published in 2002 by
Spiro Press
17–19 Rochester Row
London SW1P 1LA
Telephone: +44 (0)870 400 1000

First published by The Industrial Society 2001

ISBN 1 904298 214

Reprinted 2002, 2003, 2004, 2005
Ref: 6247.JC.3.2003

British Library Cataloguing-in-Publication Data.
A catalogue record for this book is available from the British Library.

Spiro Press USA
3 Front Street, Suite 331
PO Box 338
Rollinsford NH 03869
USA

Typeset by: Wyvern 21 Ltd, Bristol
Printed in Great Britain by: Arrowsmith, Bristol
Cover image by: Carlton
Cover design by: Sign Design
Photographs by: John Tramper

Inspirational Leadership

Henry V and the Muse of Fire

Timeless insights from Shakespeare's greatest leader

Richard Olivier

Inspirational Leadership

Henry V and the Muse of Fire

For Andy

with best wishes

from

[signature]

Praise for Inspirational Leadership

"A truly unique approach to illuminating the psychology and skills of inspirational leadership. Today's leaders will be fascinated by the story of Shakespeare's hero and will find extraordinary, and useful, parallels with their own challenges. Shakespeare and Olivier, a combination to reckon with!"
Barry Lawson Williams, CEO, American Management Association

"Fascinating insights… the Bard and Richard Olivier know a great deal about good leadership."
Charles Hampden-Turner, Judge Institute of Management Studies, Cambridge University, co-author, *Building Cross Cultural Competence* and *Riding the Waves of Culture*

"Grounded examples and telling lessons… As a bonus, it's wonderful to have such a committed and passionate author as Olivier."
Chris Knight, Chief Executive, Group Lotus Plc

"The inherited business language of present-day organizational life is far too narrow to reveal the real inner necessities and urgencies of creative leadership. The shadows are too deep and the light too dazzling to be encompassed by our jargon. In Shakespeare, Olivier finds a language and an imagination grand enough for the secret hopes hidden in our labors; the hopes for visibility and recognition, meaning and transcendence; all wished for amidst the dramas and difficulties of the every day."
David Whyte, poet and organizational consultant

Acknowledgements

To my father Laurence, who introduced me to *Henry V* at an early age, via BBC 2, most Boxing days. To the genius we call William Shakespeare. To the cast and crew of *Henry V* and all at the Globe who helped me understand and interpret the play in 1997. To Mark Rylance, Clare van Kampen and Peter Dawkins who showed me how to read the myths in Shakespeare. To my mentors Robert Bly, Michael Meade and James Hillman who taught me to explore the wisdom of stories, images and poetry. To David Whyte who inspired me to use stories in organizations. To Nicholas Janni for advice and help at many different stages. To Jacquie Drake, Andy Logan, Sandy Cotter and Mary Mills at Praxis, for supporting the work through its infancy. To William Ayot, Robert Sherman and all at Wild Dance Events for encouraging and helping to hold early Mythodrama workshops. To Ron Pyatt and Mary Aver for instilling the courage to lead. To Michael Boyle for "Sopley" and other mischief. To Malidoma Somé and Martín Prechtel for ancient wisdom and modern ritual. To Ian Gee for his absurd idea to use H*enry V* as a management text. To Claudia Heimer for taking the idea in-house to clients. To Geoff Mead who took it into police training. To Patrick Spottiswoode and Debs Callan in Globe Education for supporting the joint venture with Cranfield. To Tony Morgan and Ian Lawson for taking it into the Campaign for Leadership. To Charles Collingwood for taking it to a publisher. To Carl Upsall and Susannah Lear for commissioning, editing, advising and overseeing the text. To John Tramper for his photographs. To John Costales for designing (and redesigning) the models and charts. To all the managers and leaders who have been with me on Henry's journey into leadership. And to Shelley, who believed in me when I did not yet believe in myself.

Dedication

This book is dedicated to my family, past, present and future – in particular to Shelley, Troy and Ali.

Foreword

"May I with right and conscience make this claim?"

Shakespeare is good business for an artistic director of a theatre, whether or not that theatre is Shakespeare's Globe. His plays are commission free and people want to hear them. They want their children to hear them. People make films of them now too.

When Richard Olivier's father Laurence made the film of *Henry V* we were amazed to discover that he only used about 30% of the original text in the filmscript. The production that Richard and I worked on for the opening of the Globe Theatre in 1997 played at around three hours and we probably used 60% to 75% of the text.

Three hours is common for a Shakespeare production these days. When the actor Shakespeare was a shareholder in the Globe, the evidence suggests that plays lasted two hours. So, I believe even Shakespeare cut his plays for the audience at the Globe. I think he wanted the audience to understand him, but I don't think that was just for good business reasons. I think he wanted them to understand themselves (whilst enjoying themselves), and he thought theatre was the best way of doing that.

This was not a new idea. The classical societies, of which Shakespeare was widely read, used drama to give young men the experience of balancing their emotions and thoughts when faced wth perilous situations of leadership, before they might be faced with those situations in real life, in one form or another. In the theatre no one really gets hurt by the effects, even of a trip to the underworld of chaos. The Greeks called this training the "Orphic Mystery School". It was a school not of information but of experience. At the entrance of their temples, between the pillars of Hercules, they wrote: "Man, know thyself and thou shalt know the universe." Between the pillars on the Globe stage, Shakespeare made this kind of school available to all society.

Some of the most powerful men of Shakespeare's London came to the

Globe for two hours' traffic. One, the Earl of Essex, most notably the day before he was arrested for high treason and eventually executed. But many of the powerful men and women regularly heard Shakespeare in their own centres of business, the Inns of Court, and Whitehall itself. The detailed observation in Shakespeare of the issues facing these powerful leaders in Elizabethan society is quite remarkable. The plays are primarily about the concerns of monarchs and potential monarchs. The language and classical imagery that you rarely hear in the modern Globe, and may not have heard in the original Globe, due to cuts, would have been understood and enjoyed in the Inns of Court and Whitehall. My point is that the plays were constructed to suit their audience. Richard Olivier suits the play for leaders, and I would argue leaders in society were always an audience in Shakespeare's mind.

Of course, we all have to lead our lives, seeking inspiration and direction for ourselves and those dear to us. Some of us are also responsible for the leadership of others. Indeed, it seems whoever we are, our inspiration, our ethic, our leadership, affect the lives of others.

This book is not about presentation skills, the voice, the gesture, the spin of an actor. The mirror Shakespeare brings to any human endeavour reflects the relationship between motivation, thought and action. Dramatic experience of these three at work can help us to go forward with faith in our desires, hope from our understanding, and benefit to life in our actions.

The great German writer Goethe believed that the function of Art was to encourage the growth of the organs of insight. Insight, instinct, intuition. These are crucial and mysterious qualities in a person who beneficially leads a group. In my many experiences with Richard Olivier, he is constantly searching out and discovering the pathways to insight, instinct and intuition.

As the Dalai Lama has said, "You don't have to look too far to see that most of the problems facing humanity are man made." If we want to make a difference, it's time to look in the mirror, and Shakespeare may be the deepest mirror we have.

"Cry God for Harry! England and Saint George!" We can all cry for blessing on our simple humanity, whatever land we depend upon, and the potential of our mysterious spirit. "Once more unto the breach, dear friends, once more!" The defensive walls are high, the breach between narrow, the sweet scent of an open garden in the air. "How yet resolves the Governor of the town?"

I will always be grateful to Richard Olivier for the crucial part he continues to play in the successful re-opening of Shakespeare's Globe; for the many flashing rays of light, dark silences, roars of laughter and great sails he encourages me to hoist up the mast.

Mark Rylance

Artistic Director, Shakespeare's Globe Theatre 2001

Contents

CONTENTS

Introduction

PART 1

Henry V and leadership

THE NEW LEADER

It is increasingly common to hear people say that we are facing a crisis of leadership. The ways in which organizations are moving forward can no longer be comprehended through the same models, language and logical analysis that have served leaders in the past. The rational leader has got business where it is – they will not be able to take it where it needs to go. The leaders of tomorrow will need to be ordinary human beings with extraordinary talents.

The new leader will be both inspired and inspiring. They will be able to find and hold a vision while enthusing others to share that vision. They will be able to manage chaos and complexity while instilling enough stability to ensure smooth daily operations. They will be able to change direction at the drop of a hat (or market) from one imagined future to another – without losing the support of associates, staff, customers, suppliers and other stakeholders. And they will be able to manage creatively the emotional impact of constant change.

THE ARTS, SHAKESPEARE AND *HENRY V* IN BUSINESS

Now – perhaps for the first time in recorded history – Business actually needs what the Arts have to offer in order to survive. Creativity, imagination, flexibility, adaptability, effective communication, visionary tendencies and apparent insecurity have always been the staple diet of artists; and organizations are beginning to realize that the Arts have more to offer them than a night out or a sponsorship opportunity.

I have been working with techniques of arts-based learning for some 20 years since studying theatre at UCLA in the early 1980's. For the past six years I have developed a new form of experiential workshop called Mythodrama, which combines great stories with psychological and philosophical insight, creative exercises and organizational development techniques to explore issues faced by the modern manager.

Stories have been used to inspire and instruct human beings since we learnt how to speak. We are able to look into a story and see ourselves in its characters and its landscapes.

Of all Shakespeare's stories, *Henry V* is the one from which we can learn the most about the nature of inspiration. I believe Shakespeare wrote *Henry V* as the myth of a great leader. It is not an accurate historical picture but, as we shall see, it is a near-perfect story of successful leadership – a leadership wrought in the pyschological realism of tough decision making and personal challenge. And it is not just the famous speeches that we can learn from, but the intricate subtleties of incidents throughout the play. From the first line that calls to our imagination with its plea for "a muse of fire", to the last scene where Henry, as a victorious leader, struggles to turn a battlefield into a garden, the plot reflects invaluable insights into leadership.

Henry V unites a group of disparate people (his nobles) around a common goal (reclaiming the territory of France) and manages to overcome all difficulties in his path to achieve a near-miraculous victory against the odds (winning the battle of Agincourt). So readers are invited to see the King as an inspired leader, the nation as an organization, the nobles as a senior management team, France as a big project or territory there is reason to claim, etc. The metaphor of a *big* struggle is one that most people find easy enough to relate to their own leadership practice. (Actually invading a neighbouring country is not recommended!)

Shakespeare survives so robustly through the changing fads of every generation because he touches so consistently on the truth of human experience. In an era when it would have been unwise to stand up at Hyde Park Corner and complain about monarch and parliament, it was possible to write a play from which contemporary leaders could learn. I believe *Henry V* was, at least in part, an attempt to communicate lessons in leadership to those in power during the first Elizabethan era. Whilst

Henry's literal experience may not directly reflect our own, to the extent that this story reflects the truth of the human experience of power and responsibility these lessons are still applicable today.

So the story will act as our muse, a mirror, and a point of departure. Just as a jazz player might take a musical theme and "riff" around it, so I will use Henry's journey through the play to stimulate inquiry into what makes a leader inspirational. Not all the subjects discussed here will be found directly in the text of the play, but all have arisen in conversations and action learning sessions stimulated by the story during Mythodrama workshops.

These are often supported by real-life case studies drawn from the experience of past participants and clients. Personal and corporate identity is often deliberately disguised so I can share the genuine concerns and dilemmas of the individuals concerned without breaking confidentiality, and include descriptions of deeds and decisions some would not want attributed in a public arena.

What follows is a record of the insights that have been harvested by myself and my working colleagues, by those involved in the production of *Henry V*, and by the many managers and leaders who have participated in Mythodrama seminars.

THE STORY BEHIND THE BOOK

I came to appreciate Shakespeare's genius relatively late. Growing up as the son of the famous actor Laurence Olivier had a huge number of advantages, but being motivated to work professionally with Shakespeare was not one of them! I had chosen instead to put much of my energy into the fields of psychology, mythology and personal development.

These interests were stimulated in the wake of my father's death in 1989 by the emerging work of men's development. There I learnt to treat myths and stories from many cultures as maps of the psyche – entry points for those who chose to learn about themselves and their relationship to the world around them. It was there, also, that I had my first meaningful interactions with people from the business world. Before that business had seemed the enemy – the corporate beast that us noble-minded artists were struggling against. Now I opened my eyes and saw a different picture.

At about the same time a chance meeting with Mark Rylance (now Artistic Director of Shakespeare's Globe Theatre in London) prompted a different line of inquiry. We began collaborating on a series of workshops and soon found that, if participants allowed themselves to enter the world of a Shakespeare play, and imaginatively and physically "live through" its situations, they gained knowledge and insights not normally available to them through reading or watching the same play. It was the beginning of Mythodrama.

In 1997 I directed Mark as Henry V for the Globe's opening season and the work entered a new and more intense phase. As part of our preparation I took the cast away for two days to an abandoned airfield to improvize and "live through" the story. We also ran a workshop on the play in conjunction with the Office for Public Management. We wanted to know what, if anything, in this 400-year-old story was remotely relevant to modern leaders. We worked through the play with a group of 15 leaders and senior managers from local government, education, the police and the health service. At the end we were intrigued to hear they had got more out of Henry's journey into leadership than most management courses they had been on in the last 10 years. It seemed that we had stumbled onto something...

Other commitments meant that it was another year before I was able to return to the seeds sown. Now, some three years after that, it is a full-time career; the seeds sprouting into a Creative Management Development department at the Globe Theatre and Cranfield School of Management, my own consultancy practice, Olivier Mythodrama Associates, and this book.

MYTHODRAMA

The method is cross-disciplinary and combines theatre techniques with mythology, psychology and organizational development. The synthesis of

Acting raw behaviours in .

these four elements provides a creative and safe mirror in which participants can see their own leadership dilemmas reflected. Psychodrama is a technique that combines theatre skills with psychology to provide therapeutic interventions. Scenes from the past are re-enacted – acted out – as a way of relieving stress or trauma, often resulting in a catharsis or exorcism of negative feeling. In Mythodrama we work from the other direction; imagining and invoking characters we want to play in the future (behaviours we want to embody) and "acting them in". By putting these images in the body and trying them out, in a contained environment, we gain access to previously unimagined possibilities. It is, literally, "rehearsing" new ways of being. Just as an actor would rehearse a new character before attempting to try it on stage in front of an audience, so Mythodrama enables leaders in communities and organizations to rehearse new roles with which to meet future challenges.

TEXT AND INTERPRETATION

This is a book about *leadership*, not about Shakespeare. No prior knowledge of the play or author is required. The characters and their situations will take us on a journey that is self-explanatory. Where the text is used, it is based on an edited version of the words we ended up playing at the Globe, and more heavily edited here to give the reader a flavour of the language, rather than a surfeit. Occasionally, the text is further modified to aid understanding within the context. Past clients often say they have gone back to the play, or a film version, after working with Henry's story "mythodramatically", and got more out of it than they ever could have before.

As a director one inevitably interprets plays and the characters in them, often to reflect the particular time of a production. In 1943 my father was encouraged by Winston Churchill to make his film of *Henry V* in time to raise morale for the D-day landings. It is great propaganda, unashamedly heroic and patriotic – not a traitor in sight! Kenneth Branagh made his film after the Falklands war, and in his version war is dirty and ugly, a political necessity, full of compromise and potential dishonour. At the Globe we were celebrating a victory of the determined and visionary over the dismissive and critical. Sam Wanamaker spent 25 years raising money and awareness to get the Globe built, fighting against the odds all the time, and sadly dying two years before it was completed. When we approached our production the fact of the Globe's existence felt like a miraculous victory, just as Henry's did at Agincourt.

After discussion we decided not to opt for the heroic route, but instead to explore the human dilemmas of leadership. Just what does it take to rally a group of disparate forces around you and unite them in a common goal? How does a human being inspire others to make huge sacrifices for the sake of their vision? How can you balance the need to be seen as a leader with the natural need to express oneself as a human being? These were the kinds of questions we took with us into the rehearsal room, and the kinds of questions I have taken into boardrooms and training rooms ever since. Like many questions in this book there are no simple answers, but I will use Shakespeare's story in conjunction with the experience gleaned from working with managers and leaders "at the coalface" to shed some light on them.

PART 2

The story of Henry's past – Prince Hal

Before we meet Henry in *Henry V* we have a chance to observe him as Prince Hal, the King-in-waiting, during *Henry IV Parts 1* and *2*. His previous history gives valuable insights into what follows. Here is a brief summary of the main actions and relationships through which Shakespeare reveals his character.

HENRY IV PART 1

Hal has gained a reputation for being a hard-drinking, hard playing layabout under the tutelage of a notorious fun-lovin' criminal, Sir John

Falstaff. He spends most of his time in a tavern in Eastcheap surrounded by like minded rogues; Poins, Bardolph, Nym, Pistol, and the hostess with the mostest, Mistress Quickly.

His father, King Henry IV, having usurped Richard II from the throne some years previously, wants to launch a holy crusade to Jerusalem, but the heavy weight of civil wars keeps delaying his intention.

A young nobleman, Harry Percy, known as "Hotspur", is gaining such an honourable reputation that the King wishes Hotspur were his son, instead of Hal, who he thinks is "stained with riot and dishonour".

Falstaff plans a highway robbery of some rich pilgrims, which the Prince agrees to participate in, until Poins later persuades him to turn the tables on their friends and rob the robbers. Hal speaks directly to the audience and tells us he is playing a deliberate game. He says he is imitating the sun, which allows clouds to smother its warmth, and then is more appreciated when it reappears:

> *So, when this loose behaviour I throw off,*
> *And pay the debt I never promised,*
> *By how much better than my word I am...*
> *Redeeming time when men think least I will.*
>
> (Act 1 Scene 2, from lines 202–211)

The robbery and the robbing of the robbers goes according to plan. Hal and Poins retire to a tavern where Hal drinks with the servants, who, he says, "tell me I am a lad of mettle and when I am King of England I shall command all the good lads in Eastcheap". Falstaff returns but the drinking and joking is interrupted by a summons for Hal to visit his father. Falstaff asks Hal to role play the meeting to prepare him for a paternal chiding. Pretending to be the King, Hal says: "There is a devil haunts thee in the likeness of a fat old man". Falstaff, now pretending to be Hal, defends himself: "No my good lord, banish Nym, banish Bardolph, banish Poins, but for sweet Jack Falstaff, kind Jack Falstaff... banish not him thy Harry's company, banish plump Jack, and banish all the world." To which the Prince replies; " I do, I will" (Act 2 Scene 4 lines 467–473).

Hal meets his father, who tells him "the hope and expectation of thy time is ruined" and "thou hast lost thy princely privilege with vile participation." Hal promises to redeem his reputation by defeating the young pretender, Hotspur (who has joined the rebel forces after an argument with the King). King and Prince prepare for the forthcoming battle.

Hal wangles a position for Falstaff as head of "a charge of Foot". Falstaff takes bribes to let people avoid recruitment and admits; "now my whole charge consists of ancients... (and) discarded unjust serving men. No eye hath seen such scarecrows." When Hal complains, Falstaff replies: "Tut tut, food for powder, food for powder. They'll fill a pit as well as better" (Act 4 Scene 2 lines 10–66).

As the two sides ready for battle Hal admits he has been "a truant to chivalry" but in order "to save the blood on either side" offers to "try fortune with (Hotspur) in a single fight." The rebel leaders decline the offer and the battle begins.

Falstaff, meanwhile, decides that honour will not save his life; "therefore I'll none of it". When Hal meets him, in the heat of the battle, needing to borrow a sword, he is annoyed to find only a bottle of sherry in Falstaff's sword sheath; "is it a time to jest and dally now?"

Hal fights on and saves his father from a rebel attack. Finally he comes face to face with "Hotspur", calls him "a very valiant rebel", but asserts that England can no longer contain them both. They fight and Hal kills Hotspur.

Hal sees the prone body of Falstaff (who is playing dead to avoid the fight): "Poor Jack, farewell... I could have better spared a better man", and goes off. Falstaff gets up and congratulates himself; "the better part of valour is discretion, in the which better part I have saved my life". He looks at Hotspur's body, worried he, too, might rise again, then, realizing some potential in the situation, sticks his dagger in the dead body and drags him off. He claims Hotspur rose and fought with him for a full hour. Hal sees through the lie but, knowing sheriffs are looking for Falstaff in connection with the earlier robbery, says: "If a lie may do thee grace, I'll gild it with the happiest terms I have". He gives up his prize to protect Falstaff's liberty.

The battle is won, but not yet the war against the rebels. The King and his almost redeemed son Hal end the play with a commitment to divide their armies and pursue the rebels into their home territories.

HENRY IV PART 2

Here we meet the Lord Chief Justice, a man who has earlier arrested Hal for striking him in the course of his duty. He seeks out Falstaff to tell him: "You have misled the young Prince" (Act 1 Scene 2 line 158), and to relay an order that Falstaff's command be under Prince John of Lancaster, rather than Hal. Their separation has begun.

But Hal has not yet given up his sense of fun. He and Poins decide to disguise themselves as servants and spy on Falstaff in the tavern that night. Falstaff is drinking heavily and describes Hal as "a good shallow young fellow; he would have made a good pantler, he would have chipped bread well..." (Act 2 Scene 4 lines 228–230). The disguised Prince overhears the insult, reveals himself and berates Falstaff, who begins to invent excuses. They are interrupted by messages that the rebels are gathering once more. Hal says: "I feel me much to blame, so idly to profane the precious time... Give me my sword and cloak: Falstaff, good night" (Act 2 Scene 4 lines 349–353). It is a short leave-taking and evidence of the changing relationship between the two. It will prove to be the last time they drink together.

Falstaff leaves for the country to stay with an old acquaintance, Justice Shallow, and earn some money with his recruiting tricks. Back in the Palace the King recognizes that there is "danger and disease at the very heart of the kingdom" and acknowledges the difficulties of leadership; "uneasy lies the head that wears the crown".

Hal takes command of the army in Wales while his brother, Prince John of Lancaster, meets with the Northern rebels to hear their complaints. John promises that he will redress their grievances if they dismiss their troops. The rebel leaders agree but when their troops have dispersed he arrests them for treason.

Back at the Palace the King talks to his advisor, Warwick, of the "unguided days, rotten times and headstrong riot" he feels sure will destroy the reign of his son. Warwick suggests the Prince merely "studies his companions, like a strange tongue, wherein to gain the language" and believes "the Prince will in the perfectness of time cast off his followers… turning past evils to advantages" (Act 4 Scene 4 lines 58–77).

The battle against the rebels has gone well on all fronts but after hearing the good news the King becomes deathly ill. Hal returns to speak to his father for the last time. He hears the King's prophecy of the coming time:

> *Harry the fifth is crowned: Up vanity!*
> *Down, royal state! All you sage councillors hence!…*
> *Have you a ruffian that will swear, drink, dance,*
> *Revel the night, rob, murder, and commit*
> *The oldest sins the newest kind of ways?…*
> *England shall give him office, honour (and) might!"*
>
> (Act 4 Scene 5 lines 119–128)

Hal assures his father of his wish "to show the incredulous world the noble change that I have purposed." The King accepts his word and shares some advice:

> *Griefs are green;*
> *And all my friends, which thou must make thy friends,*
> *Have but their stings and teeth newly taken out…*
> *Therefore, my Harry,*
> *Be it thy course to busy giddy minds*
> *With foreign quarrels.*
>
> (Act 4 Scene 5 lines 181–215)

Hal accepts the crown from his dying father:

> *My gracious liege,*
> *You won it, wore it, kept it, gave it me,*
> *Then plain and right must my possession be,*

Which I with more than a common pain
Against all the world will rightfully maintain.

(Act 4 Scene 5 lines 220–224)

The King dies. The Lord Chief Justice fears "all will be overturned", especially his own career. But when Hal enters as Henry the Fifth, saying "this new and gorgeous garment, majesty, sits not so easy on me as you think", he asks him not only to remain Lord Chief Justice, but also to become his new mentor:

You shall be as father to my youth,
My voice shall sound as you do prompt my ear,
And I will stoop and humble my intents
To your well-practised wise directions.

The new King promises to call parliament and choose "limbs of noble counsel, that the great body of our state may go in equal rank with the best governed nation" (Act 5 Scene 2 lines 118–138).

Meanwhile, Falstaff is returning to London for the coronation. When he heard of Henry IV's death he boasted to his friends: "Choose what office thou wilt in the land... I am fortune's steward... I know the young King is sick for me! Let us take any man's horses, the laws of England are at my commandment, blessed are they that have been my friends, and woe to my Lord Chief Justice!" (Act 5 Scene 3 lines 120–135).

But Falstaff has not read the Prince's intentions correctly. Now he waits for the new King to pass him on his coronation procession and shouts out to him: "My royal Hal... I speak to thee, my heart". But receives an unexpected response from King Henry V:

I know thee not, old man, fall to thy prayers...
Presume not that I am the thing I was,
For God doth know, so shall the world perceive,
That I have turn'd away my former self,
So will I those that kept me company...

When thou dost hear I am as I have been,
Approach me, and thou shalt be as thou wast,
The tutor and the feeder of my riots:
Till then, I banish thee, on pain of death,
As I have done the rest of my misleaders,
Not to come near our person by ten mile.
For competence of life, I will allow you,
That lack of means enforce you not to evils;
And, as we hear you do reform yourselves,
We will, according to your strengths and qualities,
Give you advancement.

(Act 5 Scene 5 lines 40–71)

The play ends with Prince John and the Lord Chief Justice sharing a rumour that before the year is out they will "bear civil swords and native fire as far as France…"

PART 3

The story of Henry V
(and important leadership themes)

This is an overview focusing on the elements of the play that have proved most compelling when looking at the story as a leader's journey. The details of each scene can be found at the beginning of the relevant scene-chapter.

ACT 1 – FROM VISION TO COMMITMENT

Act 1 sets the scene, assesses the past, visions the future and shows Henry building consent around his mission and then visibly committing to it.

The Chorus asks for "a muse of fire" that will help us move beyond the "brightest heaven of invention". It is a call to the imagination and a

Henry's Journey

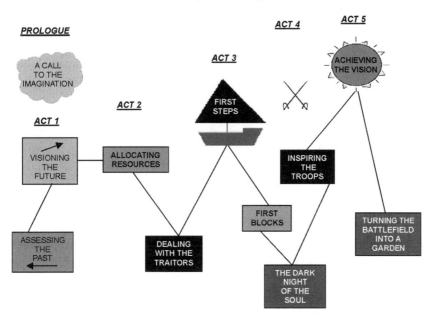

plea to the audience to not just sit passively and watch but to engage their creative faculties to help the actors "piece out our imperfections with your thoughts".

> There is a similar move happening in the world of business today. We need people at all levels of organizations to be creative, adaptable and imaginative, not to sit around and wait to be told what to do.

In the first scene we meet the Archbishop of Canterbury and the Bishop of Ely. They are assessing the past before deciding on a future. They remind us of the recent civil wars and the chequered past of the new King. However, they claim that at the moment of his father's death, "consideration like an angel came and whipped the offending Adam out of him", and since that moment he has acted like a model king.

There is a move afoot to strip the Church of some of their lands, which the bishops may avoid if they can help Henry prove that he has a claim to the throne of France.

The transition into leadership is difficult to achieve fluidly and effectively, particularly if those around you have known you for a long time. If you don't take the time to assess where you have come from, and where you are now, you may not find out where to go. New leaders can usefully seek a worthwhile project on which to cut their teeth and prove themselves. Everyone has the potential to be a leader; there is no particular past experience that mitigates for or against success.

Now we see Henry himself, meeting with his nobles to gather support for his proposed mission to reclaim the territory of France. He will not go unless it can be proved he has the *right* to go. The Archbishop demonstrates that he does. Next he must get agreement from the nobles, whose support he needs and resources he relies on. They, too, are keen to go. Henry has sent a message to King Charles of France asking if he will give up his throne. The French Ambassador arrives with an answer; a trunk which Henry assumes will be full of jewels in an attempt to buy him off. Instead it is full of tennis balls, sent by Charles's son, the Dauphin, with an accompanying message that Henry had better stick to the trivial pursuits he is capable of winning, like tennis! Henry gives the Ambassador a right-royal telling off and sends him out. Finally, he makes a visible and firm commitment to pursue the mission to France.

In starting any big project – but especially our first project as a leader – we need to seek sound advice and make sure we (and those around us) believe in the "right" to go ahead. This "right" is granted internally and externally. Internally we can use a "line of service" to draw strength from. It helps to have a Vision of a better future that the Mission (or project) is a viable first step towards. We need a certain amount of political intelligence to win the external right; to prepare our nobles (senior management) to take a risk and follow us into new territories. We will need the ability to speak confidently in public in order to face down those who doubt our ability to achieve the mission. And we will have to make a demonstrable and visible commitment to pursue the project in hand. If people think we are not totally behind the new initiative, it will probably fail.

ACT 2 – TRAITORS AND OTHER BAD HABITS

In Act 2 Henry must gather and allocate his available resources, and identify and deal appropriately with those who would oppose the mission before it has even started, especially the traitors.

The Chorus tells us of the excitement that surrounds the news of the expedition to France and the eagerness of most youth to join the struggle. But there are also three traitors – Cambridge, Grey and Scroop (Henry's Treasurer) – who have been paid by the French to kill Henry before he can set sail.

> In any major project a leader should be able to identify the forces ranged
> for and against them.

First, though, we meet Henry's old buddies in the tavern; Pistol, Nym and Bardolph. They are squabbling about women, drink and gambling debts while their erstwhile leader, Falstaff, is languishing in a sick bed. "The King has killed his heart" they say. However, they acknowledge that they must keep earning and decide to go to France for the looting.

> A leader needs to be clear about how they are going to deal with their old friends, and whether those friends have a place around the top table. On an inner level, a wise leader will also know their own "appetites", the old habits and behaviours that might get in the way of success.

Henry enters, walking with the traitors, apparently unaware of their intentions. He plays a game with them before revealing he knows of their treachery. He expresses his feeling of betrayal, and only when that has been cleared does he deliver his judgement. They are sentenced to death.

> Sometimes a good leader has to be a good actor. We will have to hide certain knowledge from certain people at certain times. We may need to disguise our intentions, particularly when attempting to identify those who disagree with the agreed mission and who may oppose the desired outcome. There are different types of "Disagreers"; I call them Naysayers, Critics and Traitors. They exist in most organizations. It is important to identify them correctly and deal with them appropriately. If we do not

recognize the emotional impact of dealing with the "Disagreers", we may make judgements based on subjective rather than objective criteria, and lose the trust of others around us. Sometimes an apparently harsh judgement saves a lot more trouble later.

ACT 3 – INTO BATTLE; FIRST FOOTHOLDS, FIRST SETBACKS

Act 3 sees Henry taking the first steps into France, meeting the first blocks to success, overcoming them, staging a strategic withdrawal and ending up surrounded by a vastly superior force, to whom he is asked to surrender or die.

Henry starts with a reasonable plan. Arrive in August with 10,000 troops, take the first foothold in a week and march on to Paris by Christmas. He lands at the coastal town of Harfleur as planned – but three months later he is still there, having lost 2,000 men. He makes a rousing speech to his exhausted troops.

> However grand the vision or the mission, they must be a practical place to start. When things get stuck – especially when it is not the troops' fault – an effective leader will have to speak passionately and imaginatively to motivate them through the blocks.

The next attack seems to make a difference, for the Governor of Harfleur asks for a peace parley. Henry speaks and warns that if the town is not surrendered now he will be unable to control his troops' anger. Then, when they do succeed, the town will be destroyed and the people abused and killed. The Governor surrenders the town. Henry insists that all the inhabitants be treated mercifully. He changes strategy and decides to withdraw to Calais (an English territory at the time) where his troops can rest over winter.

> Throughout the play Henry demonstrates the wonderful leadership quality of painting pictures of the future. Here he uses it to paint such a negative view of the future that the Governor gives in rather than risk that picture becoming reality. He does not press on to his initial goal regardless; he

revises his strategy on the ground. Nor does he admit failure and simply retreat to England. He finds a third way, a strategic withdrawal.

During the withdrawal Bardolph (one of Henry's old friends from the tavern) is caught stealing, an offence for which he is due to be hanged. Henry agrees that the sentence should be carried out. The French army is chasing Henry's exhausted 8,000 walking men with 40,000 fresh mounted troops. Inevitably they catch up and surround the English on the field of Agincourt. The French Herald is sent in to offer Henry a simple choice. Give in now (and pay a huge fine but Henry and all his troops live), or fight tomorrow and die. Henry says he does not seek a battle at the moment, he wishes to march to Calais, but if challenged he will fight. The French prepare for battle.

> Managers have to solve problems, leaders have to manage dilemmas; complex issues with no happy solution. They will need to balance Justice against Mercy and Truth against Loyalty many times. Any seriously important project will have a crisis, a point at which it seems impossible for the originally desired outcome to occur. That is when a leader meets the real test. They will need to call on all their skills to hold a line that will give their people enough confidence to carry on.

ACT 4 – THE "DARK NIGHT OF THE SOUL"

Act 4 shows Henry going through the long dark night before the battle, facing up to his fears and duties before being able to inspire his troops to an apparently miraculous victory, against the odds.

The Chorus tells us that the English are waiting, like ghosts, to die. At three o'clock in the morning Henry walks around, visiting all his troops, "thawing cold fear".

> Sometimes the acting makes it real. Henry cannot really want to be out talking to his troops at three o'clock. But he does it because it is required of him. He exercises visible leadership. He is seen by others, and he sees them, thus bolstering confidence.

Henry tells his brother, Gloucester, "we are in great danger". He is asked to meet with his nobles but says no; "I and my bosom must debate awhile and then I would no other company". He takes off his crown, puts on a cloak and walks about unrecognized. He enters a conversation with some ordinary soldiers who believe they will die, and that if they do not die well "it will be a black matter for the King that led us to it". He ends up challenging one of them to a fight, if they both survive the battle. Left alone he unloads some of the burden of leadership that he feels; "what infinite heartsease must kings neglect that private men enjoy?" He ends with a confessional prayer. Now he feels ready to rejoin his nobles and prepare for battle.

Leaders need to allow themselves to enter the "dark night of the soul" and face their own innermost fears, doubts and uncertainties, especially in a crisis, and especially before they make decisions that affect the lives of others. If they don't, they may make the wrong decisions for the wrong reasons. There is a point in most meaningful projects when we are forced to ask ourselves: "Is this the right thing to do?" and "Am I the right person to do it?" In these times we will have to manage our own fears and the fears of others simultaneously but differently. We need to put on a brave face for the troops, but equally important is our inner reality. Henry finds a brother with whom he can share his private truth. He then takes "time out" to reflect on the difficult situation they are in.

Henry is courageous enough to listen (in disguise) to what the troops really think. And they, like troops in crisis the world over, are blaming the boss. But if he listens carefully to what they are thinking, he may just be able to inspire them later. However, he also feels the weight of responsibility that many workers project onto their leaders. He needs to unload this or he may make his decision based on what others want, rather than what he thinks is right. Finally, when he prays, he faces his own inner demons. Now he is ready to go back into the fray.

When Henry arrives back at his tent he overhears the nobles wishing for more troops. He speaks to them from the heart, telling them why he, personally, believes they are doing the right thing. He says they are enough to win honourably or die trying. He says those that do not wish to fight can leave, but any who choose to fight and who survive will remember this day for the rest of their lives. He calls them a "band of brothers" and promises that those who miss the fight will regret it later. The French Herald returns with another offer of surrender which Henry roundly refuses. They go off to start the battle.

> The whole process of surviving the "dark night" has served to strip away layers to reveal Henry's centre, his core values – what he is doing all this for. And it is from this core that he speaks to inspire others.

The battle is going well for the English. They deal with the first wave of French attack and capture many prisoners. Another attack is sounded. Henry orders his men to kill their prisoners. Meanwhile the French have raided the luggage tents and killed all the boys who were guarding them. The Herald enters and tells Henry the day is his. He thanks God and forbids anyone to boast of the victory. They set off for Calais.

> Most leaders wish they could get through their career without having to take any of the really tough decisions. Very few get their wish. There is usually a situation in which our innocence dies – in which we are forced to compromise the values on which we prided ourselves when we started our journey into leadership. It is the ability to take these hard decisions and live with the consequences that separates the "men from the boys" among leaders. Having survived this final initiation, Henry is not naïve enough to claim credit for the victory. It happened because it was right, they did not "do" it.

ACT 5 – TURNING THE BATTLEFIELD INTO A GARDEN

In Act 5 Henry is encouraged to make peace and turn the battlefield into a garden. He attempts to court Princess Katherine but realizes he has much to learn about building relationships before the political necessity becomes a heartfelt reality.

Henry is warned by the Duke of Burgundy of the dangers of continuous conflict. If the fighting continues, the "garden" of France that he fights for will be destroyed. Henry attempts to court the Princess, but he is not a fluent suitor, he has "an aspect of iron" which he finds difficult to take off. Katherine agrees to the marriage but he can tell she does not yet love him. Burgundy advises him to be patient, to change his approach and to learn a new way of being over a long summer. Henry agrees to try, and the engagement is sealed.

Many leaders have got where they are because of their ability to fight and win. Sometimes, though, this is not enough. We may have to nurture the new territory we have achieved, rather than look for the next target. If we never take the "armour" off and build real and lasting relationships the work may eventually lose its meaning. As the phrase goes; no one on their deathbed ever said "I wish I'd spent more time at the office!"

It is never too late to adapt our habitual styles. The older we get the longer it may take to unleash, but if we find the motivation we all have boundless potential.

Prologue

A call to the imagination

Left to right: Henry V (Mark Rylance), Duke of Exeter (Matthew Scurfield), Director (Richard Olivier), Duke of Gloucester (David Lear) in technical rehearsal for *The Life of Henry the Fift* at the Globe Theatre, May 1997.

CHORUS   *O for a muse of fire, that would ascend*
           The brightest heaven of invention...
                    But pardon gentles all
           The flat unraisèd spirits that hath dared
           On this unworthy scaffold to bring forth
           So great an object...
           And let us, ciphers to this great account,
           On your imaginary forces work.

Prologue

A call to the imagination

CHORUS *O for a muse of fire, that would ascend*
The brightest heaven of invention:
A kingdom for a stage, princes to act,
And monarchs to behold the swelling scene.
Then should the warlike Harry, like himself,
Assume the port of Mars, and at his heels,
Leashed in like hounds, should famine, sword, and fire
Crouch for employment. But pardon, gentles all,
The flat unraisèd spirits that hath dared
On this unworthy scaffold to bring forth
So great an object. Can this cock-pit hold
The vasty fields of France? Or may we cram
Within this wooden O the very casques
That did affright the air at Agincourt?
O pardon: since a crookèd figure may
Attest in little place a million,
And let us, ciphers to this great account,
On your imaginary forces work.
Suppose within the girdle of these walls
Are now confined two mighty monarchies,
Whose high uprearèd and abutting fronts
The perilous narrow ocean parts asunder.
Piece out our imperfections with your thoughts:
Into a thousand parts divide one man,
And make imaginary puissance.
Think, when we talk of horses, that you see them,
Printing their proud hoofs i' th' receiving earth;
For 'tis your thoughts that now must deck our kings,
Carry them here and there, jumping o'er times,
Turning th' accomplishment of many years

3

Into an hourglass—for the which supply,
Admit me Chorus to this history,
Who Prologue-like your humble patience pray
Gently to hear, kindly to judge, our play.

THE STORY

The first Chorus of *Henry V* exhorts us to use our imaginations to help the actors tell their story. It begins by wishing for "a muse of fire". A muse was the spirit of inspiration and the source of genius for those involved in the creative process. The image of fire rises up to the heavens and burns away whatever is in its path – both compelling to watch and dangerous to touch, like all creative inspirations. What is desired is that the muse of fire will rise further than anything the world has yet seen – "to ascend the brightest heaven of invention".

COMMENT

I believe this is a timely call to those who hold leadership positions today. We have recently crossed the threshold into the third millennium of our Common Era and such landmarks give us the opportunity to think more broadly than usual. At the end of a decade we usually think about the last 10 years and the next 10, at the end of a century we consider a hundred years back and forward, now, uniquely for the last 40 or so generations, we can ponder the next 1,000 years. What is it that we human beings want for our world and our future? Like it or not, business is what makes the world of our daily life go round. So what is it that business in general, and organizational life in particular, can offer that world and that future?

As I hope to show, one of the prerequisites for inspirational leadership is the ability to think in terms of the bigger picture, to imagine beyond simple material profit to what serves the community at large. We will need leaders who have access to a "muse of fire" if we are to contend constructively with the huge implications of the information revolution

4

and globalization. I believe we are living in a period that will come to be seen as a second Renaissance. In Shakespeare's time the printing press was revolutionizing the flow of information, and the "brave new worlds" of newly discovered lands offered potential for both constructive and destructive exploration. Our time has seen the creation of the world wide web and the expansion of multinational conglomerates, both of whose reach and influence extend far beyond that of any national government. Whether these developments will prove ultimately constructive or destructive for our planet remains to be seen.

"Brave new worlds" require brave new leaders who are prepared to inhabit brave new roles. One such role is played by the Chorus – the ability to call out creative and imaginative responses from those around them. The leaders of tomorrow will be saying: "We cannot do this alone, we need your help, your input, your imagination, so that together we can envision the future". And it will rarely be one single linear future that will be envisioned. There will be many possibilities, dependent on many variables, both internal and external, company, market and community driven, that will have to be divined, juggled and chosen by those at all levels in organizational life.

All of which will require people at work to be more creative, flexible and adaptable than in the past. This is why arts-based training and creative consulting have been such growth areas in management development recently. Those in business are being required to learn the skill sets more generally associated with artists. Artists have for centuries dealt with multiple possibilities, worked from an empty page and managed the uncertainty of not knowing. Now it's your turn.

Let this Prologue then, like the first Chorus, be a call to the imagination of each reader. This book, like Shakespeare's play, means little without you and your imaginative response. It is your thoughts that now must deck these pages and clothe the ideas with your own insights, to give them life beyond the written word.

The word "imagination" shares the same root as "image", "magic" and "magi" (as in the three wise men). We will be working with images throughout the book; to stimulate your own magic and wisdom; to discover, perhaps, a "muse of fire" that can "ascend the brightest heaven of invention".

As Einstein wrote: "Imagination is more important then knowledge – for while knowledge points to all that is, imagination points to all there will be..."

Act 1

From vision to commitment

Left to right: Bishop of Ely (William Russell), Archbishop of Canterbury (John McEnery), Duke of Exeter (Matthew Scurfield), Lord Scroop (Steven Skybell), King Henry V (Mark Rylance), Duke of Bedford (Nick Fletcher).

Photo: John Tramper

After being insulted with a "present" of a treasure chest full of tennis balls from the French Prince, the Dauphin, Henry makes a visible commitment to his nobles to pursue the proposed mission to reclaim the territory of France:

> *We are glad the Dauphin is so pleasant with us.*
> *When we have matched our rackets to these balls,*
> *We will in France, by God's grace, play a set*
> *Shall strike his father's crown into the hazard...*
> *But tell the Dauphin I will keep my state,*
> *Be like a king, and show my sail of greatness*
> *When I do rouse me in my throne of France.*

ACT 1 • Scene 1

Assessing the past

THE STORY

The play itself begins with the Archbishop of Canterbury and the Bishop of Ely waiting outside the King's council chamber, discussing the recent past and assessing its implications for the present.

There is a move afoot by some nobles to pass a bill stripping the Church of many lands and privileges, to pay for the recent ravages of civil war and internal dissension. Their best defence would be the King, who, Canterbury states, is "full of grace and fair regard", though a little while before they would not have thought so:

The courses of his youth promised it not.
The breath no sooner left his father's body
But that his wildness, mortified in him,
Seemed to die too. Yea, at that very moment
Consideration like an angel came
And whipped th' offending Adam out of him,
Leaving his body as a paradise
T' envelop and contain celestial spirits...

ELY   *We are blessèd in the change.*
CANTERBURY *Hear him debate of commonwealth affairs,*
You would say it hath been all-in-all his study;
List his discourse of war, and you shall hear
A fearful battle rendered you in music;
Which is a wonder how his grace should glean it,
Since his addiction was to courses vain...
His hours filled up with riots, banquets, sports,
And never noted in him any study,
Any retirement, any sequestration
From open haunts and popularity.

9

Having thus expounded their King's newfound leadership talents, they return to the bill in question. The Archbishop is seeking to save the Church lands by supporting the King to embark on a different mission, to enforce his claim to the throne of France and reunite the two countries (as they had been 100 years before). They wait to be called in to the King's presence to present their case.

TELLING THE ORGANIZATION'S STORY

In many organizations there is hardly time for lunch, let alone assessing the past. Yet food, both literal and metaphorical, is important. Appropriate reflection is the nourishment that feeds our future. Without it, how can we be sure of the ground from which we wish to move forward? As the saying goes: "If you don't know where you have been, or where you are, how the hell can you know where you want to go?"

Of course, there will be the practical assessment. We will know the figures, and the statistical analysis against the projections. But how often do we take time to tell the story of the past? Not the result but the process, not the "what" but the "why" and the "how"? Wherever we are and whatever we do, we are all, always, part of a story. Human beings have always passed on knowledge this way; stories are storehouses of wisdom that can teach and inspire us. There is not a day goes by that we do not tell, hear, read or see a story, from children, partners, friends, or the media. But we go to work and start reporting facts and speaking in acronyms. A leader who does not know what story he or she is in, and where they are within it, is missing an essential route to inspiration.

HONOURING PAST ACHIEVEMENTS

A colleague at Cranfield, Jacquie Drake, recently asked me to join her for a piece of work with the senior management team of a large railway engineering project. The team was a third of the way through a five-year project, head down in chaos, doing something no one had ever done before, faced with pressures, deadlines and a budget they did not know they could meet. Expensive mistakes were beginning to surface; as the MD put it: "Would you employ a plumber who took all your old pipes out, and then told you he didn't know how to put the new ones in?" Naturally, they wanted to focus on the present and the future: "What are we doing wrong today and what can we do better tomorrow?"

But as they began to engage with Henry's story we asked them to pair up and, like the bishops, share their stories of the past. Where had they come from individually and as a project team? What were the struggles they had already survived and what learning had already been achieved?

When we pooled their stories, the energy in the room began to change. Words were used like "pride" and "success", and phrases such as "making a difference", "setting a standard", "leading in our field". At the end of the session there was a sense of achievement present that had visibly lifted their spirits. No one person in the room had known all there was to know about the past. And now, simply from hearing the story of past learning and success, they felt reassured in their capacity to overcome future challenges. They decided to have the story written up and presented to others not present who were involved in the project and in need of a boost.

An effective leader will need to tap into any available source of inspiration – and one is past achievement. The inspired leader keeps an eye on the bigger picture and can remind people of the past to motivate efforts for the future.

THE BEGINNINGS OF LEADERSHIP

Some of the seminars I run on *Henry V* work specifically with managers stepping into a leadership role for the first time, just as Henry does at the end of *Henry IV Part 2*. These participants often feel, like Henry, that "this new garment (leadership) sits not so easy on me as you think". Questions arise such as "What makes a leader?" and "How can I lead people who used to be my peers?" The answers to these questions are more individual than general – each new leader will have their own unique journey to take into leadership – but there are some common themes.

A primary requirement is ambition. (Actually, *appropriate* ambition, for we don't have to look far elsewhere in Shakespeare – *Macbeth, Richard III, Coriolanus* – to find over-ambitious leaders who turn into tyrants.) If you do not wish to be a leader after due consideration you will probably be better off out of it. "Will I be up to the challenge?" is a natural question, but if, deep down, you lack the conviction that you have something to offer you will probably fail. Timing is important too. I believe there are windows of opportunity in life and these windows open and close at certain times. Henry, as the young Prince Hal, reveals both his ambition to lead and his decision to wait for the right moment to shine:

> *(I will) imitate the sun,*
> *Who doth permit the base contagious clouds*
> *To smother up his beauty from the world,*
> *That, when he please again to be himself,*
> *Being wanted, he may be more wondered at...*
> *So, when this loose behaviour I throw off,*
> *And pay the debt I never promised,*
> *By how much better than my word I am...*
> *My reformation, glittering o'er my fault,*
> *Shall show more goodly, and attract more eyes,*
> *Than that which hath no foil to set it off.*
>
> (King Henry IV Part 1, Act 1 Scene 2)

The word "ambition" comes from "ambit"; the Greek root also means "wingspan", the space between wingtip and wingtip. In other words, how far we can stretch our wings. If we never open the wings we will never fly, if we stretch them too far we may crash to the ground, as often happens to high flyers.

An "ambit" was also the journey that a king or queen would take each year to walk the perimeter of their territory. This was partly to restate their claim to the territory, but principally to be seen to be the leader by the people. Now, if a monarch laid claim to more territory than they could comfortably per-ambulate in a year, they would have no time to do anything else (which is one reason why the over-ambitious are so prone to burn out). Metaphorically we can ask these questions of the leadership challenges we may be offered: "Is this within my wingspan?", "Do I have the right to claim this territory?" The answers may well be more intuitive than scientific. If it feels like an appropriate challenge, fine; if not, proceed with caution.

"LEAVING THE TAVERN"

Another favourite question of emerging leaders is "How do I leave the pub?" – referring to Henry's transition from one of the lads to a respected king. It may not be easy but it is necessary. However much we may de-layer and seek consensus a leader can never be just "one of the lads". A leader needs to be – even if it is just a bit – "more equal than others". This does not mean we have to sever all old friendships, often quite the opposite; when you become a leader you find out who your real friends are, but a certain separation is inevitable. Apart from anything else your old friends will now need a little space to whinge about the boss – you!

> I once coached the Managing Director of a small publishing company, John, who had spent 15 years working his way up the company ladder. He prided himself on keeping in close touch with old colleagues from every rung he had climbed. But now the firm was facing a crisis, prompted by e-commerce rivals and desktop publishing. He had clear ideas about how to move forward, but no one accepted them. They all argued the toss about every decision, just as they had when he had been their peer and every decision was up for grabs. He still went out to the pub with a bunch of colleagues every Friday, where he would be publicly chided for not sorting out the mess.
>
> We talked through Henry's treatment of his old friend Falstaff at the end of *Henry IV Part 2*. Once Henry has taken the throne he deliberately creates distance between them. When Falstaff shouts to the new King during his coronation, calling him "my sweet boy", Henry replies:
>
> > *I know thee not, old man, fall to thy prayers...*
> > *Presume not that I am the thing I was,*

For God doth know, so shall the world perceive,
That I have turn'd away my former self,
So will I those that kept me company...
I banish thee...
As I have done the rest of my misleaders,
Not to come near our person by ten mile.
For competence of life, I will allow you,
That lack of means enforce you not to evils;
And, as we hear you do reform yourselves,
We will, according to your strengths and qualities,
Give you advancement.

So, the possibility of future advancement, a small pension, but distance and banishment from within 10 miles of Henry's presence. John said: "He's a hard bastard – he's betrayed his mates, left them behind". Perhaps, but if he promoted a bunch of thieves to high office, that would be a betrayal too, but with potentially greater consequences.

The fact is that you are probably going to have more fun if you stay in the pub, but not the same chance to make a difference. If John continued on his current path his business would continue to suffer and eventually he would probably lose most of his mates anyway. He needed to take his authority and gain some respect if he wanted things to change.

After more discussion John decided to call an extraordinary meeting of all employees, where he would publicly state the difficulties they were in, set out his plans, and ask for a commitment to move forward together. He would also let them know he would no longer be coming to the pub every Friday. But when they had turned the business around he would buy them all a drink.

THE ANGEL OF CONSIDERATION

In the play it is clear that Henry's past had left senior management severely concerned about his leadership potential:

14

CANTERBURY   *His addiction was to courses vain,*
              His companies unlettered, rude, and shallow,
              His hours filled up with riots, banquets, sports,
              And never noted in him any study,
              Any retirement, any sequestration
              From open haunts and popularity.

But something radical and fundamental happened at the moment of his father's death, as Canterbury reports:

> *The breath no sooner left his father's body*
> *But that his wildness, mortified in him,*
> *Seemed to die too. Yea, at that very moment*
> *Consideration like an angel came*
> *And whipped th' offending Adam out of him,*
> *Leaving his body as a paradise*
> *T' envelop and contain celestial spirits.*

The time of a parent's death is often a defining moment in our lives. A wake up call to adulthood and responsibility – taking the next step up the family tree. In Henry's case it is also the time for his promised reformation – the moment he stops being Prince Hal and becomes King Henry V.

A similar change occurs in many leaders. While we have less responsibility we take the chance to play, but when opportunity knocks, we are able to stop and take the responsibility it appears we previously neglected. When the old leader "dies" and we become the leader, some youthful, irresponsible part of us "dies" as well. Sometimes those who play hard, particularly those able to mix with diverse people, excel in leadership roles. There are few past behaviours that "prove" candidates ineligible to lead.

"Consideration" came to whip the offending Adam out of Henry. The "Adam" in Renaissance times was the greedy instinct for selfish personal survival that ignores the needs of others. To "con–sider" means to think with and on behalf of others. Consideration is a requirement of effective leadership. If we are not willing and able to think with and on behalf of others we might ask "What's in this for me?" rather than "Is this the Right Thing for us to do?" (As the current cliché puts it; "Managers do Things Right, Leaders do the Right Things.") Right Things can only ever become clear after consideration.

To put it simply, without this "angel of consideration" Henry may never have left the tavern. But he was touched by this "angel", was able to change his old behaviours and open up to the spirit of inspiration. Most of us are not so lucky. It may take us years to figure out what the behaviours are that get in our way, let alone get rid of them. Often what finally moves us is the sense that we will miss out on something important. Our potential, or possibly, our destiny.

THE SENSE OF DESTINY

The words "destiny" and "destination" share the same linguistic root. Destiny can be thought of as our destination in life. Where is it we could be headed? The psychologist James Hillman makes an important distinction when he talks about destiny as a "calling". Most of us, if we ever think about it at all, wish to find our destiny in a moment and remain connected to it for ever – as if we were to get on a train and ride along to a clearly identifiable station. But it is not that easy. Hillman encourages us to think about the journey more like a small yacht crossing an ocean. We head out in a general direction and are blown back and forth, so we have to tack across the desired path, rather than being attached to it. The moments we are actually dead on course are few and far between. The only signs we get are when we are too far off course, when we feel stuck, confused or lost. In the end we are lucky if we wind up in the continent we were aiming for, let alone the port we set out towards! But, as the poet David Whyte says; "if you can see more than one step ahead of you, it is not your path". If you are looking at a clearly marked path, someone else has laid it. It cannot be your unique and emerging way.

THE LINE OF SERVICE

This can sound rather high flown, fine for princes certain to inherit a kingdom but not relevant to the rest of us. But I believe that all inspirational leaders are themselves inspired by something beyond themselves and their ego. They seem to share a sense of service. Albert Schweitzer once told a group of reporters: "I do not know what your destiny will be, but one thing I do know. The only ones among you who will be truly happy are those who have sought and found how to serve." Over the last three years I have developed a "line of service" for Henry.

Henry's Line Of Service

"Angel of consideration"

Sense of purpose/Destiny

Vision

Mission/Project/"France"

First steps

This line is a suggestion rather than a prescription. We can move up and down it, and the stages are not necessarily sequential. Henry's journey into leadership started with an "angel of consideration". But this in and of itself is not enough. We all know people capable of thinking with and on behalf of others, but unless they *do* something about it they are not leaders but dreamers.

So the "angel" needs to be connected to the sense of having a destiny or a purpose. Feeling that there is something that we could be doing that would be the "right thing" for us to do. George Bernard Shaw in his play *Man and Superman* puts it like this: "This is the true joy in life; the being

17

used for a purpose recognised by yourself as a mighty one. The being a Force of Nature – not a feverish, selfish little clod of ailments and grievances constantly complaining that the world will not devote itself to making you happy".

The key here lies in the self-recognition. There are many people around who may tell us what we should be doing; parents, teachers, bosses, peers, the media, *et al*. But when we find "*it*", we know, because it feels right. Motivation then comes from within. We want to work towards achieving this purpose because of the feeling that it is what we are supposed to be doing. The sense of purpose makes the effort meaningful. When it is absent the chances are that we will complain that "the world does not make us happy", often back in the tavern.

VISION

Once we have found a connection to a sense of purpose the next question becomes: "What do I do about it?" The sense of purpose opens a space inside of us where vision can grow. David Whyte catches this idea in his poem *What to Remember when Waking*:

> *...You are not*
> *a troubled guest*
> *on this earth,*
> *you are not*
> *an accident*
> *amidst other accidents*
> *you were invited*
> *from another and greater*
> *night*
> *than the one*
> *from which*
> *you have just emerged.*
>
> *Now, looking through*
> *the slanting light*
> *of the morning*
> *window toward*

the mountain
presence
of everything
that can be,
what urgency
calls you to your
one love? What shape
waits in the seed
of you to grow
and spread
its branches
against a future sky?...

Definition of vision.

The realization that "You are not an accident" is akin to finding the sense of purpose; the "shape that waits in the seed of you" is the potential vision. I define vision as a desired future; something that can make a positive difference, does not yet exist, but is not impossible. When shared it helps to unify others around a goal and motivate them.

There is a (probably apocryphal) story about Kennedy and NASA that illustrates this. When the Russians launched Sputnik, Kennedy was inspired to go on national television to announce his vision that America would put a man on the moon within a decade. Unfortunately he had not checked with NASA first, who, at that time, were simply incapable of doing this. However, the vision caught the popular imagination, resources were made available and the space race speeded up. Some time later Kennedy was visiting the NASA site to boost morale. He met the staff, lined up in a corridor. At the end of the line he was introduced to the toilet cleaner, who, when asked what his job was, replied proudly; "Mr President, I'm helping put a man on the moon". Probably not the first thought that would normally spring to mind in that job. A powerful and memorable vision is a powerful motivator.

MISSION

The Mission, then, is a practical way of putting the Vision into action; an actual project that can hit the ground.

VISION + ACTION = MISSION

If a mission does not have a vision to serve, it becomes much more difficult to motivate oneself as a leader and the troops when things get tough. If the vision has no mission, it will remain in the air, a good idea without application. A vision is more internally driven, a mission more externally. If the vision is being achieved you feel it, if the mission is being achieved you can measure it. *Yin Yang*.

HENRY'S LINE OF SERVICE

Let's trace Henry's line of service. His mission (big project) is to reunite the countries of England and France. We know that at the end of the play that mission has been accomplished – it is written in a treaty and is measurable. His vision – which remains implicit rather than explicit in the play – would be to serve his people and his country to the best of his ability. (At the end we probably feel he is on track to achieve this vision but we could not prove it.) I imagine his sense of purpose to be a strong belief that he is supposed to play an important part in the history of England. And the "angel of consideration" is the inner prompting that nudged him out of the pub in the first place.

The Bishop of Ely says: "We are blessèd in the change." People who work with leaders committed to a line of service often feel a sense of "blessing". Such leaders have access above and beyond the task at hand and remind us of the meaning behind the work. We often want leaders to tell us what to do and how to do it, but those who can truly inspire others will also communicate the *why*.

ACT 1 • Scene 2

Vision, mission and commitment

THE STORY

King Henry V is meeting with his nobles in an effort to turn his vision into a mission and to reclaim the territory of France. He asks the Archbishop of Canterbury to make the case for his claim to the French throne, but warns him:

> *Take heed… how you awake our sleeping sword of war,*
> *For never two such kingdoms did contend*
> *Without much fall of blood.*

The Archbishop reports that, according to Salic law, no one can claim through a feminine line, as Henry is doing, but his research has shown that at least three French kings have done exactly that. His moral right in reinforced by the bible where "It is writ 'when the man dies let the inheritance descend unto the daughter'".

Canterbury advises Henry to pursue his claim, advice supported by the majority of the nobles, including Henry's cousin, Westmoreland:

> *Never King of England*
> *Had nobles richer and more loyal subjects,*
> *Whose hearts have left their bodies here in England*
> *And lie pavilioned in the fields of France.*

Henry reminds them that they must not forget to defend their existing territory:

> *We must not only arm t' invade the French,*
> *But lay down our proportions to defend*
> *Against the Scot, who will make raid upon us*
> *With all advantages.*

21

As an argument builds between the nobles about how or if they will be able to achieve both, the Archbishop reminds Henry of his role as leader to oversee many apparently contrary actions and to bring them under one overarching frame:

> *Therefore doth heaven divide*
> *The state of man in divers functions,*
> *Setting endeavour in continual motion;*
> *To which is fixèd, as an aim or butt,*
> *Obedience. For so work the honey-bees,*
> *Creatures that by a rule in nature teach*
> *The act of order to a peopled kingdom.*
> *They have a king, and officers of sorts,*
> *Where some like magistrates correct at home;*
> *Others like merchants venture trade abroad;*
> *Others like soldiers, armed in their stings*
> *Make boot upon the summer's velvet buds...*
> *   I this infer:*
> *That many things, having full reference*
> *To one consent, may work contrariously.*
> *As many arrows, loosèd several ways,*
> *Fly to one mark, as many ways meet in one town...*
> *So may a thousand actions once afoot*
> *End in one purpose, and be all well borne*
> *Without defeat.*

Henry then calls in the messengers sent from the Dauphin, Prince of France, to know the official response to his claim. The Ambassador delivers the Dauphin's gift, a box of tennis balls, and message; that Henry should stick to the trivial pursuits he is capable of winning (ie tennis) and not bother real leaders further. Henry answers the message:

> *We are glad the Dauphin is so pleasant with us.*
> *When we have matched our rackets to these balls,*

We will in France, by God's grace, play a set
Shall strike his father's crown into the hazard...
And we understand him well,
How he comes o'er us with our wilder days,
Not measuring what use we made of them...
But tell the Dauphin I will keep my state,
Be like a king, and show my sail of greatness
When I do rouse me in my throne of France.

He dismisses the Ambassador, demanding he be given safe conduct, and then has to rally his nobles around his vision. He makes a visible commitment to launch the project:

My lords, omit no happy hour
That may give furth'rance to our expedition;
For we have now no thought in us but France,
Save those to God, that run before our business.
Therefore let our proportions for these wars
Be soon collected, and all things thought upon
That may with reasonable swiftness add
More feathers to our wings; for, God before,
We'll chide this Dauphin at his father's door.
Therefore let every man now task his thought,
That this fair action may on foot be brought.

WHY DO WE NEED A VISION?

Not much happens without a dream. And for something great to
happen, there must be a big dream. Behind every great achievement
is a dreamer of great dreams. Much more than a dreamer is required to
bring it to reality; but the dream must be there first.

(Robert K Greenleaf, The Servant as Leader)

I believe that Shakespeare presents Henry V to us as an example of a

23

great leader pursuing and achieving a great dream. Like many leaders, Henry's actions are open to interpretation; an opposing point of view is entirely possible. So Henry could be a young hungry leader who manipulates his advisors to tell him what he wants to hear and seeks to end internal differences by invading a common (and popular) enemy. In other words, an aggressive takeover bid. TYRANTS

Some seminar participants are reluctant to even enter the conversation about vision. This is typically due to past experience of bullying tyrants who impose their views on others regardless. So we need to make a crucial distinction between those whose primary goal is to serve themselves and their career and those who genuinely seek to improve the common good; to leave the world a better place.

I hope to show that Henry belongs to the latter category, but it can be difficult to distinguish between them. Some of the actions and behaviours will be the same. The difference between inspiration and manipulation is often as simple as whether you agree with what is being said. Imagine sitting with a friend watching a political party conference. If one of you supports the party in question, and the other opposes it, the chances are that the supporter will feel inspired and the opposer manipulated by the same words being spoken by the same person. The difference is whether you believe it.

One of the difficulties of standing up for a particular dream is that some people will assume you are trying to manipulate them for your own advantage. If that thought embarrasses us then we may avoid situations where this energy is called for. So we deny ourselves the opportunity of living a big dream and may just sit around complaining that there are no inspiring leaders nowadays. But, in the words of the great German writer Goethe, "Whatever you can do, or dream you can, Begin it! Boldness has genius, power and magic in it. Begin it now!"

VISION MAKES A DIFFERENCE

In seminars, when I ask people to decide what Act of the play most interests them, the majority usually go for Act 4 – surviving the "dark night of the soul" and inspiring the troops. I then point out that the only way to survive the dark night is to have a clear sense of why you started your big project in Act 1. If you don't know how the project is serving a vision, there will be no way through to the light of dawn.

Another colleague, Danah Zohar, was sent the following:

VISION:

Is seeing the potential purpose hidden in the chaos of the moment, but which could bring to birth new possibilities for a person, a company or a nation.

Vision is seeing what life could be like while dealing with life as it is.

Vision deals with those deeper human intangibles that alone give ultimate purpose to life.

In the end, vision must always deal with life's qualities, not with its quantities.

It is the clearest statement I have come across that gives a sense of what vision actually means. It was sent to Danah by a client, Sven, whom she had helped through his own particular "dark night" experience.

Sven was a senior manager at a large fast food company in Sweden. He loved walking in nature, was becoming ecologically and environmentally aware, and was becoming increasingly disturbed at the amount of his company's polystyrene fast food wrappers he saw whenever he went for a walk. Eventually he got to the point where he thought he could not continue to work for a company that was, however unconsciously, contributing to the pollution of the environment in this way. He met Danah for a lengthy coaching session after which they defined three main choices. He could quit and go and live on top of a mountain where, all being well, he would never have to look at another burger wrapper again. He could quit, form his own environmental consultancy, and sell his services back in to any organization that shared his values. Or... he could stay where he was and make a difference.

   After much soul searching he decided on the latter. At last report he is now working at his firm's corporate headquarters, in charge of a project to design the world's first environmentally friendly fast-food-container factory. He is developing a process to make containers out of potato starch: the material is 100% biodegradable and will dissolve into the earth in time. His vision includes sharing the technology so within 10 years there need be no polystyrene fast food boxes polluting the natural environment anywhere in the world. Whether his company will endorse that part of his vision remains to be seen...

It would probably have been easier for Sven to take one of the first two options and, in effect, walk away from the problem. To stay and fight takes courage and determination, and connection to a line of service. Sven realized that the mission he had been pursuing on behalf of his company was not in line with his vision and his personal values. He decided to do something about it. Many people in similar situations turn a blind eye, compromise their values and stay. Some leave and find work more in line with their beliefs. Very few pull the company into alignment with their personal vision.

BE AWARE – BE OPEN

Vision is seeing the potential purpose hidden in the
chaos of the moment, but which could bring to
birth new possibilities for a person, a company or a nation.

In our current and probable future working environments a certain amount of chaos is inevitable. Old predictable patterns have given way to emerging possibilities that must be sought out and acted upon before all the relevant information is known. For many traditional managers this is a frightening prospect; "Aren't we being paid to stop chaos?" But if we do this we will never see the "potential purpose hidden in the chaos of the moment". We may eradicate the chaos but with it we stamp out the potential purpose.

Henry is faced, at the end of the scene, with a box of tennis balls – a completely unexpected response from the Ambassador. He has been pulling his nobles together and impressing them with his reformed character when, suddenly, he receives a public slap in the face. He has to respond out of the chaos of the moment, but turns it to his advantage with a rousing reply:

> *We are glad the Dauphin is so pleasant with us.*
> *When we have matched our rackets to these balls,*
> *We will in France, by God's grace, play a set*
> *Shall strike his father's crown into the hazard...*
>   *And we understand him well,*
> *How he comes o'er us with our wilder days,*
> *Not measuring what use we made of them...*
> *But tell the Dauphin I will keep my state,*
> *Be like a king, and show my sail of greatness*
> *When I do rouse me in my throne of France.*

This is the first time that Henry publicly claims his past has been of use and the first time he lays claim to "my throne". The exchange serves to further impress those around him. If Henry had sought to control the situation he might have seen the Ambassador in private, limited the potential damage of public humiliation, and missed the opportunity that he was able to create in the moment.

So if we wish to be open to new possibilities we need to be aware of the unexpected ways in which they can surface. If we limit creative thinking to officially designated "brainstorm sessions" we may miss the great idea we almost had on the way to the coffee station. As the American manager and writer James Autry puts it:

RECESSIONS

Why do we keep on keeping on,
in the midst of such pressure,
when business is no good for no reason,
when everything done right turns out wrong,
when the Fed does something
and interest rates do something
and somebody's notion of consumer confidence does something
and the dogs won't eat the dog food?

What keeps us working late at night
and going back every morning,
living on coffee and waiting for things to bottom out,
crunching numbers as if some answer
lay buried in a computer
and not out among the people who
suddenly and for no reason
are leaving their money in their pockets
and the products on the shelves?

Why don't we just say screw it
instead of trying again,
instead of meandering into somebody's office
with half an idea,
hoping he'll have the other half,
hoping, what sometimes happens will happen,
that thing, that click, that moment
when two or three of us
gathered together or hanging out
get hit by something we've never tried
but know we can make work the first time?

Could that be it,
that we do all the dull stuff
just for those times
when a revelation rises among us
like something borning,
a new life, another hope,
like something not visible catching the sun,
like a prayer answered?

Personally, I love the move Autry makes from the everyday drudgery; computers and numbers and coffee – into vision – revelation, new life, something not visible catching the sun. That is what vision feels like when it strikes. We suddenly see something that may have been there all along, but only now does the light of our conscious attention reveal it to us. And if we are not aware that these spontaneous moments of possibility exist, they simply pass us by. If, as a leader, we don't encourage those around us to share their crazy ideas, we may miss out on their unexpected genius.

HEAD IN THE CLOUDS, FEET ON THE GROUND

*Vision is seeing what life could be like
while dealing with life as it is.*

We probably all know a few crazy visionaries – those people who corner us at cocktail parties and regale us with their vision of how to change the world, make a fortune, whatever. Often if we meet these types twice we find an all-new improved vision on second meeting. By the third meeting we walk across the room to avoid them.

I have worked in the field of personal development for 12 years and one of the most frustrating experiences was working year after year with some of these folk who would show up armed with a different great idea every year – and remain fatally unequipped to do anything about it. They could not get beyond the idea precisely because they had not taken this statement on board. They were only dealing with life as they wanted it to be and totally ignoring life "as it is".

The vision of the future may well be a quantum leap away from the present reality, but if we don't live and work with the present reality we will never change it.

The trick is to be able to hold this apparent paradox – see the vision *and* deal with the reality – without losing sight of either.

When the nobles are ready to run out the door on their way to France, Henry keeps their feet on the ground:

29

> *We must not only arm t' invade the French,*
> *But lay down our proportions to defend*
> *Against the Scot, who will make raid upon us*
> *With all advantages.*

Some leaders have this gift naturally, others can learn it. Once we become aware of it we simply need to figure out a way of remembering it at crucial moments. It requires what I call a third position, what actors call the ability to "third eye" yourself while you are performing. In theatre this means that a good actor is able to judge the effect of their acting on the audience while appearing to be totally involved in playing their part. In the presentation courses we run at the Globe Theatre we call this "developing dual attention". In this context it is the ability to focus on present and desired future simultaneously.

ACCESSING DISCRETIONARY EFFORT

> *Vision deals with those deeper human intangibles that alone give*
> *ultimate purpose to life.*

Intangible – you cannot touch it but you know when it is there. When we ask people about their peak working experiences the single most common denominator is a sense of purpose in what they are doing. It is this that gives leaders the most direct access to "discretionary effort"; the effort we do not have to give at work (we all know what we *have* to do to get paid) but *can* give if we choose, and if we are inspired. Discretionary effort can make the difference between real success and scraping by in a project or on a team.

In our scene Westmoreland tells Henry he will have access to this extra effort:

> *Never King of England*
> *Had nobles richer and more loyal subjects,*
> *Whose hearts have left their bodies here in England*
> *And lie pavilioned in the fields of France.*

When people's hearts are engaged with what they do, they will always do it better. Charles Collingwood, at the Industrial Society, came across a modern example.

> Charles used to be in the hotel business and, one day, while staying at a large hotel in Ireland, he noticed an unusually high level of caring service. He quizzed the manager who replied that he could not tell him exactly what was going on, but he promised Charles that everyone knew, and attempted to live, the vision. In fact, he added, if Charles could find any employee who did not know it, he would give him a bottle of Scotch. Charles never won the Scotch, but he did learn the vision. It was simply: "We are ladies and gentlemen serving ladies and gentlemen." That's all it was, but it was remarkably effective. If an employee takes this vision to heart and acts as if they are a lady or a gentleman, and treats everyone they meet at work as a lady or gentleman, they will naturally deliver excellent service. It gives them an image of how to behave and a caring manner that taps into discretionary effort and produces a desired result.

QUALITATIVE NOT QUANTITATIVE

> *In the end, vision must always deal with life's*
> *qualities, not with its quantities.*

It is hard to quantify "We are ladies and gentlemen, serving ladies and gentlemen." It would not be possible to measure if the hotel had achieved a 5% reduction in ungentlemanly behaviour in the last six months, for instance.

Other hotels would typically set themselves a hard target; to reduce customer complaints by 10% in six months, or something similar. If I were in charge of this project I would get a list of customer complaints and sort them out, one by one. So if complaints were about dirty glasses and late bellboys, I would go to the kitchen and demand all glasses be washed twice, then go to the bellboys and give them a rocket (or if I was feeling particularly generous, employ some extra help). All of which is focusing on external activity not internal behaviour. In the Irish hotel it was not what was being done but *how* it was being done that made the difference. By improving the quality, the quantity took care of itself.

DON'T CONFUSE THE VISION WITH THE TARGET

As we identified in Henry's line of service, the Vision stands behind or above the Mission. It adds the "why" to the "what". There has been a lot of work done with organizations on vision statements in recent times; to the point where it is almost a cliché. But in my experience many of these statements fail to add the "why" to the "what".

A couple of years ago I was invited by a colleague, Claudia Heimer from Ashridge Consulting, to use *Henry V* as the frame for a top team to work on issues around vision, strategy and leadership. They ran the UK manufacturing division of a global food and drink company. We started by assessing their current vision and mission. They reported that both were well on track, although the bulk of their employees did not share their sense of success. The mission was "To maintain 10% growth for the next three years", and the vision "To become a half billion pound a year company by 2005". We wondered how excited their employees were supposed to be by these statements, and asked the team if these words got them out of bed in the morning. They said no, not in and of themselves, but once they were out of bed they knew what they were aiming for. Fine, we said, so what you have are targets. Crucial to have but important not to confuse with the inspirational possibilities of vision. Both statements reminded them "what" they were doing, not "why".

A vision comes out of a desired future connected to quality; the team's statements may have been effective strategic intent, but they were purely quantitative. We facilitated a more qualitative discussion around personal values, and asked each individual to identify what is was that got them up in the morning. What, apart from the money, inspired them to work for this company? When these were shared there were, inevitably, some agreements and some unique points of view. Since the team were genuinely concerned that their employees started feeling better about the company and their future, we took it a stage further. We asked the MD and the newest member of the team to summarize and distil the important elements of the previous discussion. This finally crystallized into a single phrase: "Great people winning with inspiring products." The team felt happy with it. Not to replace the other statements, but as a way of enriching them. They wanted their people to feel good about coming to work, and to be proud of their products (and to keep winning). This process of arriving at the new statement had changed the energy in the room. People said it had inspired them.

"Inspiration", after all, comes from the word "in–spirare", to breathe in. And a vision is like a breath of fresh air, it gives energy. On a subtle level I would say that the fundamental ability of an inspirational leader is to change the energy in those around them. And one of the most effective ways of doing this is to have and to hold a vision that means something to those who will have to put it into action. If you have this then you have something to draw on in the hard times.

I was asked to work with the management team of a children's charity, who were 18 months into a two-year project but had only raised 15% of their target. Naturally, the team felt as if they bashing their heads against a brick wall – 75% of time gone, only 15% of funds raised. But every day they went to work with that thought foremost in their heads was a day in which they would find it very difficult to motivate others. We spent our time on Henry's journey reconnecting them to the vision that had moved them to set such an ambitious target in the first place – the welfare and safety of children. If they could get up with that thought foremost in their heads for the next six months they would have a much better chance of motivating others to help them get as close as possible to the original target. When things get bad we all tend to focus on the target it appears we will fail to meet. An inspirational leader needs to rekindle the flame of the vision *behind* the target.

FINDING A VISION

Take a moment to think where you are with this. Do you currently feel inspired in what you do? If so, can you put that inspiration into words? If not, have you had a vision and lost it, or never had one?

Vision can work on many levels, organizational, departmental, team and personal. Group visions can help gather people around a common goal, as did the example above. They involve give and take from all concerned, as it is unlikely that any one person will come up with words everyone else agrees to. It is best as a team effort, where everyone feels they have contributed and been heard.

Leaders may have a vision they wish to share with others and this needs to be done carefully. If it is once rejected, it is hard to return to it with the same people. If others feel imposed upon it can even have a negative effect. If the values behind the vision (and the reason for it) are carefully explained, and space is given for reactions and comments, a leader's vision can be accepted (or marginally adapted) by a larger team. Individual visions do not have to be shared with others, but sometimes the troops may just need to know what gets you out of bed in the morning for a particular project, especially in a crisis (as we shall see in Act 4).

Defining an individual vision that makes sense takes time. It is hard to do under pressure, and impossible to do properly with a deadline. There is no right way to arrive at a vision, some arrive in moments of blinding clarity, and others emerge slowly, when they are ready. The elements may be there for a long time before the whole picture is clear. Others change over time as their owners refine them through experience. I use one particular exercise when working with individuals, that combines two lines of inquiry – one from core values, one from analyzing the past.

Think about your own experience... Consider your core values. What is it that you really care about in your life? What types of things, habits, people, behaviours, activities and situations do you tend to gravitate towards? And what do you avoid or move away from? A list of both of these will usually offer a few common themes that may not have struck you before.

Now think about your past. Track back through your life and identify the times when you felt closest to inspiration and vision, and the times you felt furthest away from it. What was going on at those times, who was around, what were you doing, how did you feel, etc? This should provide a few useful signposts.

From this general field it is then possible to select a few themes, words and phrases that strike you as significant, and begin to weave a sentence together. Ben Thompson McCausland from the Industrial Society holds that an effective vision should be memorable, communicable, achievable, inspirational and *not* measurable. I agree.

The vision that inspires me at the moment is "Promoting creative inquiry into ethical and sustainable leadership, in communities and organizations." It emerged over the course of a year or so, thinking back through the work experiences that I most connected with and enjoyed. Now it helps guide me through some of the choices I have to make about work. Does this particular opportunity serve this vision or not?

Another individual vision that emerged from a recent workshop in a social services department was "Empowering others to make their own decisions and create a culture of opportunity."

A team vision developed by the management group at a chemical plant was "Making a difference, delivering improvement and taking pride in achievement." A middle management team in an entertainment company came up with "Leading as we would be led." When you find something that works for you, you know it. Then you have to live with it.

OUTER AND INNER ALIGNMENT – PICKING THE RIGHT FIGHT

The next step is to ensure that the project or mission is in alignment with the vision and that you, as leader, are sufficiently inspired by both. For Henry it is not enough to know that his senior management team will support the proposed mission, he needs to feel that he has the *right* to lead them in it. As he says to the Archbishop of Canterbury:

Take heed how you impawn our person,
How you awake our sleeping sword of war,
For never two such kingdoms did contend
Without much fall of blood, whose guiltless drops
Are every one a woe...

He is not looking simply to pick a fight, he wants to pick the right fight. That is, a fight he has a right to pick. This implies a choice that few people in organizations may feel they have, but it is important to consider nonetheless. The "right" to pursue a particular project, what some like to call a "BHAG – a Big Hairy Audacious Goal", can be granted internally and externally. Ideally we need both in order to start out with the best chance of success.

The external right comes from others and objective analysis of the situation: "Does this seem like the right thing to do?" Henry asks his spiritual advisor, the head of the Church, if he has the moral and legal right to pursue his claim over France. His right is reinforced by this external advisor in no uncertain terms:

Gracious lord,
Stand for your own; unwind your bloody flag;
Look back into your mighty ancestors.
Go, my dread lord, to your great-grandsire's tomb,
From whom you claim; invoke his warlike spirit.

Henry's personal sense that he has a right to "stand for his own" is the internal reinforcement of his claim. Without this he will not be able visibly to commit himself to a course of action with confidence. The internal right is one we grant ourselves; as Henry did at his father's deathbed:

You won (the crown), wore it, kept it, gave it me,
Then plain and right must my possession be,
Which I with more than a common pain
Against all the world will rightfully maintain.

(Henry IV Part 2, Act 4 Scene 5)

INNER ALIGNMENT – DO WE HAVE AGREEMENT "WITHIN"?

One of the most interesting methods we can apply to working with stories is "internalization". That is, we can imagine that all the characters in the story are also present within each and every one of us. In other words, we all, potentially, have a "Henry" inside of us, the leader in waiting, and an "Archbishop", an inner advisor, the one who judges whether we have the right to embrace a dream. (We will also have an inner "Falstaff" who would rather bunk off and have a drink, and inner "traitors" and various others; but we will deal with these later.) These "characters" are often played out in life as the conversations we hold in our heads. The Inner Leader might say "I should put myself forward to lead this project because I feel ready to handle a big challenge"; the Inner Advisor might reply "On the other hand, so-and-so is more qualified and can get teams working together more easily than me so maybe I should hold back and learn a bit more first."

Metaphorically, then, before we start our audacious project we need our "Henry" and our "Archbishop" to be in agreement. If one is out of balance or being dragged along unwillingly it will have serious implications later. If the "Henry" in us takes over and heads off into the breach to prove himself without checking out the "right" to the claim, we may fail to win external support when we need it. If the "Archbishop" takes over and convinces us we "should" do such and such without the inner leader really feeling it is the right thing to do, we will never be able to inspire others when the going gets tough. Alignment happens when the right "thing" (outside) is linked to the right "feeling" (inside).

WHAT IS YOUR "FRANCE"?

"We have now no thought in us but France."

In seminars participants are asked to come up with a mission that they feel they have a right to pursue, that they can hold up as a mirror to Henry's journey. The metaphorical question is "What is your 'France'?"

This can be a real project that they are already engaged in or about to start, or an imagined project that they may like to start in the future. Rather than simply regarding Henry's journey as a case study, it becomes an imaginative springboard to bounce projects off as the journey progresses. You may wish to do the same.

> Take a moment to think. Is there a "territory" you can identify that you have a right to claim that you are not currently in possession of? Is there a big project you are considering or managing that might be useful to look at through the metaphor of "Henry's journey"? If there is nothing current you can think of, would you like to imagine one?

In seminars recent "Frances" have ranged from practical targets such as "My department will exceed its quota this quarter" and "We will open three new retail outlets within 12 months", to more general aims such as "Improving interdepartmental communication" and "Overcoming resistance and installing the new intranet on schedule".

A PERSONAL LINE OF SERVICE

My mission this year is "Write this book", while the vision above that project is "Promoting creative inquiry into ethical and sustainable leadership, in communities and organizations." As a mission the book is quantifiable. Legally I have to turn in between 40,000 and 80,000 words to get paid. The vision is what I trust will add the quality to the book. Any 60,000 odd words will not serve the vision, though they would fulfil the legal (quantitative) requirement.

> When I track up the line of service I can pinpoint a time which gave birth to the above. I was running a week-long men's development seminar about eight years ago in which a number of participants were revealing the extent to which they had been damaged by their organizations. They felt used up and thrown away, squeezed dry and discarded, like so much cannon fodder or machine parts. It was a fascinating challenge to provide the space in which these men could release their pent up frustrations and emotions and

attempt to reorient themselves to go back into the world with some confidence and/or sense of purpose. As the event progressed I received a brief visit from the "angel of consideration". For the first time in my life I began to think about working in an organizational environment. Thoughts emerged like; "OK, so here you are helping to patch up the walking wounded — but what would it be like to try and really make a difference, to go upstream and work directly with those making the decisions and creating the cultures in which these wounds occur?" As I pondered these thoughts over a period of months, I began to feel a sense of purpose emerge. I saw that the tools I had at my disposal — directing ability, theatre training techniques, personal development, psychology, mythology and group facilitation — offered a fairly unique skills set with which I could meet the challenge ahead.

The question around purpose for me started very much as a conditional one. An "as if". In other words; "if there was a purpose in this particular toolkit being applied to this particular challenge, what would it be?" Although it was not a deliberate process at the time, there was a discernable line of service that led to my current "France" — this book.

PREPARING THE GROUND FOR THE MISSION

It is one thing to imagine a project, it is quite another to sell it to others. We often hope that if an idea inspires us, it will surely inspire others. The reality is that you are likely to be competing for airtime with other ideas and if you don't prepare the ground carefully your ideas may never see the light of day. Every new leader is going to be under scrutiny, so how we initiate our first big project is often the first visible test. It requires a certain political intelligence; the willingness and ability to use politics to get things done. Whether you like it or not, if you are in an organization you are in a political game. Whether you play or not is your choice. But the choice *not* to play has serious implications. Particularly if you want your project to get the green light.

Henry does not meet his nobles in Act 1 Scene 2 saying; "I've got a great idea — let's go to France!" because it would be too much of a shock, out of the blue, and besides, others will have their own agendas. He lays the ground carefully. By the end of his coronation in *Henry IV Part 2* his brother John is able to say:

> *I will lay odds that, ere this year expire,*
> *We bear our civil swords and native fire*
> *As far as France: I heard a bird so sing,*
> *Whose music, to my thinking, pleased the King.*

(Act 5, Scene 5 lines 107–110)

By the beginning of *Henry V* Canterbury and other nobles are already on board. Henry has won them over, despite their previous doubts that he could be an effective leader. He immediately showed them he was serious by banishing Falstaff during his coronation march. He started his reign with a commitment to listen first, when he asked the Lord Chief Justice to act as a mentor:

> *You shall be as father to my youth,*
> *My voice shall sound as you do prompt mine ear,*
> *And I will stoop and humble my intents*
> *To your well-practised wise directions.*

(Henry IV Part 2, Act 5 Scene 2)

It is politically intelligent to listen to those who have moved in the corridors of power longer than you; see how things are done, watch and learn.

A colleague in police training, Geoff, told me how he had to learn this lesson the hard way. He arrived at his first job full of bright and innovative ideas – and succeeded in alienating almost all of the people whose support he would eventually need. The impression he gave was that everything they had been doing for years was woefully inadequate and quite probably a waste of money. Not surprisingly, the powers-that-be resented this impression and therefore resisted all the "improvements" that he was attempting to initiate.

Luckily, Geoff gained the ear of a senior officer who was to become a mentor figure, and who called Geoff in for a private meeting after a couple of months. His opening statement was; "I have been watching you operate since you arrived and I have one question for you. Do you always want to be right – or do you want to get something done around here?" As the implications of continuing to be "right" and failing to get anything done sank in, Geoff decided to accept some wise advice before pitching in with more bright ideas. Two years later he was able to initiate and see through a major revision of training for high potential officers that has continued for some 10 years since.

SEEKING OUT SUPPORT

Canvassing – notplus inspection,

Shakespeare does not show us Henry actively seeking support in Act 1. It is implicit in the nobles' support of the proposed mission that they have had time to digest it beforehand – Henry has checked it out with them first.

> When I rehearsed the Globe production of *Henry V* we camped out for two days on an abandoned airfield to improvize and "live through" the whole story. The actors were invited to imagine and try out previous action and offstage scenes. In the prelude to Act 1, Mark Rylance (the actor playing Henry) instinctively spent a lot of time discussing his proposal before calling the meeting that takes place in Act 1 Scene 2. He spoke to his senior nobles and advisors, usually in private: "If I was to suggest going to France what would you think? Is it the kind of project you could support? If not, why not?", etc. It was only when he knew he had enough support that he called the public meeting.

This approach has several benefits. You start to get a genuine idea of whether others are going to follow you or not – and if not you can save yourself the embarrassment of a public rejection. You start to share ownership of the mission – a crucial step in trickling motivation down from the top. And you enlist support before you begin in public. If others are already emotionally invested in the project (and some may simply be pleased to have been consulted) they will be more likely to continue to support it in public.

We conduct a poll during seminars to test what internal responses people have in meetings. The conclusion is that if the first three vocal responses to a new proposal are negative, even those who started off with the possibility of being convinced tend to be swayed against the initiative. A kind of "three strikes and you're out" syndrome – only with your dream up to bat. So we need to ensure that one of the first three responses is a positive, supportive voice. *Having a ringer.*

Some people feel it would be "cheating", like having a "ringer" in the crowd; I think it is plain common sense. Most of us are – at least slightly – initially resistant to new ideas that will bring change and, if the idea is not quite so new, the chances are the resistance will not be quite so much. As the American writer James Baldwin put it: "Most of us are about as eager to be changed as we were to be born – and go through our changes in a similar state of shock!" Anything you can do to reduce the shock will help.

INHERITING A MISSION

Henry's nobles have been well prepared and are more than ready to support the proposed mission to France; indeed, some of them have been hoping for such a project for some time (the theme of going abroad has recurred throughout *Henry IV*). Some might say that Henry inherited an obligation to go – his father's last words included the instruction "Be it thy course to busy giddy minds with foreign quarrels"; which brings us to a very different stumbling block. Many of the leaders I work with would love to have the freedom to create their own way forward but have inherited a project from a predecessor that they may not feel so invested in. In public services this can be more extreme. One group of newly promoted police inspectors said: "What on earth is the point of us having a vision or a mission when the Home Secretary is going to turn round every year or so and give us a new one?" At the time I was working with a chief superintendent who responded quickly; "that is exactly why you need a more personal vision, to sustain you through the times when the organization as a whole may be struggling to come to terms with some new shift."

If there is no part of the larger vision you can stand for, and no part of the current mission you can support, you may just be in the wrong place at the wrong time. It may be time to consider other options. The urge for security may compel you to stay, and you will probably be able to fake support for a while, but in the long term it will drain you of any inspiration and meaning at work A connection to the larger vision, on the other hand, can sustain you through some of the bad times.

I recently worked with a senior manager at a major telecommunications firm who had been tasked with downsizing 10% of his division of 3,000 people. The particular downsizing mission he did not care for or believe in; his description of it was "the CEO trying to win back the confidence of the shareholders by appearing ruthless". He was a people person and had spent a long time building up the division he headed. Now, in an apparently arbitrary move, he was going to lose 300 people he valued. He was in two minds as to whether or not he should join the 300 and jump ship. After discussion he realized that the overall direction of the company was enough in alignment with his values that he was prepared to ride out short-term discomfort for the sake of long-term job satisfaction. What clinched it was his sense of loyalty to the 2,700 who would remain.

If you are going to stay and inherit another's vision the important thing is to find the piece of it that you can believe in and stand up for that. If you can't find a piece you can support you will never effectively be able to use the vision to inspire others.

In our work with the team who created the vision "Great people winning with inspiring products", it was apparent that individuals had different phrases that they personally felt more committed to. The MD wanted to focus on "inspiring products", raise the product standard and instil a sense of pride among the workforce. The HR Director wanted to focus on "great people" and enable employees to feel valued. The marketing manager was determined to keep "winning". The fact that they did not all agree did not threaten the vision. The diversity of interest actually helped create different levels of meaning and engagement with it. Each member of the team applied it in the way that was most appropriate to them and they were all able to support the whole.

BUILDING CONSENT

Once Henry has made his public pitch to the nobles they almost inevitably start squabbling over the details. Who is going to be responsible for what? What resources are required? How many troops should go on the new mission and how many stay to protect existing territories?, etc. Canterbury points out that it is the leader's job to gather different interests around a common goal:

> *Many things, having full reference*
> *To one consent, may work contrariously.*
> *As many arrows, loosèd several ways,*
> *Fly to one mark, as many ways meet in one town,*
> *As many fresh streams meet in one salt sea,*
> *So may a thousand actions once afoot*
> *End in one purpose, and be all well borne*
> *Without defeat.*

He uses the example of a beehive to illustrate his point. On the surface it looks as if the soldier bees "armed in their stings" are opposed to the merchants "venturing trade abroad". But from the point of view of the King at the centre of the hive, all are helping to fulfil the same purpose, the continuing healthy functioning of the whole.

But while each division goes about their task it is only the leader who can maintain this overall perspective. (Although some choose to employ consultants who, like the Archbishop – only more expensive – attempt to do it for them.) Some of these divisions will inevitably come into conflict, whether it is over resources, personnel or schedule. The effective leader has to build consent among dissenting divisions. It is like

Let all see overall picture.

taking someone up to the top of a mountain so they can see a whole wood that is being harvested, rather than stay fighting over a couple of trees. If people see the bigger picture their level of awareness is raised to consider the "one purpose" they all are serving. Then they may just let go of the petty disagreement, and work together to "bear all without defeat".

VISIBLE COMMITMENT

Henry finishes Act 1 with a strong statement of intent:

> *My lords, omit no happy hour*
> *That may give furth'rance to our expedition;*
> *For we have now no thought in us but France,*
> *Save those to God, that run before our business.*
> *Therefore let our proportions for these wars*
> *Be soon collected, and all things thought upon*
> *That may with reasonable swiftness add*
> *More feathers to our wings; for, God before,*
> *We'll chide this Dauphin at his father's door.*
> *Therefore let every man now task his thought,*
> *That this fair action may on foot be brought.*

He demonstrates unshakeable determination that transmits itself to all who witness it. He is not saying "We'll think about it", he is saying "We'll do it". If we wish to inspire others to follow us we will need physically to inhabit our mission. This means feeling confident about our right to move forward and expressing it with energy and passion.

In seminars it is noticeable how many people find it hard simply to stand and state their mission with conviction. But if it looks as if we are not totally committed to our own project, why the hell should anyone else commit to it? The visible commitment contains an energy that is palpable to those witnessing it and can have an almost magical effect; as WN Murray of the Scottish-Himalayan expedition noted:

Until one is committed, there is hesitancy, the chance to draw back, always ineffectiveness. Concerning all acts of initiative (and creation) there is one elementary truth, the ignorance of which kills countless ideas and splendid plans: that the moment one definitely commits oneself, then Providence moves too. All sorts of things occur to help one that would never otherwise have occurred. A whole stream of events issues from the decision, raising in one's favor all manner of unforeseen incidents and meetings and material assistance, which no one could have dreamed would have come their way.

To me, this is a bit like an image of raising a flag up a flagpole. When people see clearly what it is, and who is raising it, they can decide if they want to support it. If they never see it clearly, or sense that the person raising it does not quite believe in it, they will back off, or at best be luke warm in their response. Don't give them that option.

ARE WE "IN LINE"?

> We have no thought in us but France,
> Save those to God, that run before our business.

This is Henry's one qualification. He calls himself back to his line of service. It is as if he were saying; "the *only* thing that could sway us from our commitment to this project is if we realized that the mission was not in line with the vision."

I experienced this dilemma with a group of British police recently. This constabulary had done their best to take on board the recommendations of the Stephen Lawrence Report and combat "institutional racism". One of their new missions was to build a community centre where they could meet local youths, play football, table tennis, etc, and generally come into contact in a non-confrontational way. Sounds great. The trouble was that the crime rate was going up and the local community now felt less safe than they had before the project started. The mission had so involved and stimulated everyone around it that the core purpose of "Making Britain safer" was no longer being served. The mission, however noble, had got out of line with the vision and the core purpose was suffering. Those concerned had to rein in the runaway mission and re-focus in order to serve the core purpose – Henry's "God" that must "run before".

"REASONABLE SWIFTNESS"

> ...all things thought upon
> That may with reasonable swiftness add
> More feathers to our wings.

Shakespeare often brings two apparently opposing images together to enhance our understanding of both. Here he gives us two different energies that a leader must balance to move a project from inspiration into action; reason and swiftness. Each of us will probably prefer one or the other, the effective leader needs both. Some people get caught up in the reason; the analysis and the logical planning, but we may never receive all the information we want and if we do not incorporate swiftness at the right time we may miss the boat.

Others prioritize swiftness and can't wait to move into action. But if we do no reasoning first we will probably trip over our own feet on our rush to get out the door and get started. The people we manage will also have their favourite option and we will have to balance these energies appropriately.

SHARE OWNERSHIP

SHARING THE VISION

> ...let every man now task his thought
> That this fair action may on foot be brought.

A bit of 15th century empowerment. We would probably expect a king at that time to say the equivalent of "Right that's the vision, now I'll go and sort out the strategy and tell you what to do". But a leader who seeks to maintain their identification with a project at the expense of sharing ownership will cut themselves off from the very support they need. Henry is wise enough to know that if he wants others to invest themselves in the project he has to share it with them. There is no more effective way of doing this than to get them involved in planning the next steps.

Act 2

Traitors and other bad habits

Left to right: Guard (David Fielder), Cambridge (Craig Pinder), Grey (Christian Camargo), Henry V (Mark Rylance), Lord Scroop (Steven Skybell), Exeter (Matthew Scurfield).

Henry tricks three traitors into demanding a heavy sentence for a minor infringement of the rules by a drunk and then turns the tables, reveals he knows of their treachery, and sentences them:

> *Hear your sentence.*
> *You have conspired against our royal person,*
> *Joined with an enemy proclaimed...*
> *Wherein you would have sold your King to slaughter...*
> *His subjects to oppression and contempt,*
> *And his whole kingdom into desolation.*
> *Touching our person seek we no revenge,*
> *But we our kingdom's safety must so tender,*
> *Whose ruin you have sought, that to her laws*
> *We do deliver you. Get ye therefore hence,*
> *Poor miserable wretches, to your death.*

ACT 2 • Chorus

Inner resources, inner traitors

CHORUS   *Now all the youth of England are on fire,*
           And silken dalliance in the wardrobe lies;
           Now thrive the armourers, and honour's thought
           Reigns solely in the breast of every man.
           They sell the pasture now to buy the horse...
           O England!— What mightst thou do,
           Were all thy children kind and natural?
           But see, thy fault France hath in thee found out:
           A nest of hollow bosoms, which he fills
           With treacherous crowns; and three corrupted men—
           Have, for the gilt of France—O guilt indeed!—
           Confirmed conspiracy with fearful France;
           And by their hands this grace of kings must die,
           Ere he take ship for France.
           The sum is paid, the traitors are agreed...

FORCES FOR AND AGAINST

In order that "fair action may on foot be brought" we must assess and allocate our resources – inner and outer – and we must identify the "traitors" – inner and outer. What do we already have on our side that, if directed appropriately, will help us achieve the desired goal? And what have we not yet clearly seen that might stop us?

We will address the outer issues when we enter the action of Act 2. Here we will focus on the inner characters; the "inner resources" and the "inner traitors". Inside each of us what "youths are on fire with honour in their breasts" bursting to help us move forward? And – equally important to identify – what "corrupted men with hollow bosoms" wait to stab us in the back before we even set sail on our mission?

51

A NEW MODEL OF LEADERSHIP POTENTIALS

I have developed a model of leadership potentials that I use with Henry's journey. It is drawn from the work of several "post Jungians"; those who are implementing the ground-breaking work of Carl Jung in bringing imagination and archetype to the study of psychology. The model is most closely based on the work of Gareth Hill, a clinical social worker and Jungian analyst from Berkeley, California, found in his book (now sadly out of print) *Masculine and Feminine – The Natural Flow of Opposites in the Psyche*. I have adapted this research to focus on the roles and characters we can inhabit as leaders at work. These have both positive and negative possibilities; we'll start with the positive (see diagram below).

INTRODUCING THE CHARACTERS

We meet four characters; the Medicine Woman, the Great Mother, the Warrior and the Good King. These are created by combining the four

Positive Leadership Potentials

Good King	FIRE	Warrior
ORDER	(Doing)	ACTION
Static Masculine		*Dynamic Masculine*
Great Mother		Medicine Woman
NURTURE	(Being)	CHANGE
Static Feminine	WATER	*Dynamic Feminine*

archetypal energies of the model – the static and the dynamic with the feminine and the masculine in their different possible combinations. They are *not* gender specific. All human beings have access to all four energies and all four characters. Each individual will, however, have preferences about the characters they play. Just as an actor may prefer a certain type of part (villain, hero, love interest, friend, etc) we will also have a preference for the roles we play as leaders.

We can also look at the model as a natural cycle of life that can be applied to a human being, a plant or a project. New life starts when the dynamic and the feminine energies meet and combine to produce the Medicine Woman. This is where things are "seeded", where new ideas are born, where people and organizations go to be healed. It is a place of Change and emergence, the natural home of vision and imagination. And some of us are most happy, inspired or comfortable when we are involved in this type of activity. But, of course, seeds and new ideas do not emerge fully formed, they need to be (metaphorically and literally) watered and move into a place of Nurture.

This is where the feminine and the static energies meet and combine to produce the Great Mother, or the Earth Mother character. Here we find protection and build trust. This is as important for an idea or new project as it is for a seedling plant or a new baby. We need new things to be held until they are ready to forge their way into the world; we need to build relationships – whether to the new way of doing things or with the new team that we will be doing them with. This is an environment that holds and mirrors back our potentiality and our potency – what we are and what we can offer. Here a relationship is valued solely for the sake of the relationship itself, not for what can be got out of it. And some of us will be most happy when "playing" this character and helping others. But eventually things, ideas and people need to move into Action.

This is the shift into the character of the Warrior, when the dynamic and the masculine energies meet to produce the archetype of the dragon slaying hero. This is where the child leaves home to start a life outside the family of origin and where the plant breaks through the surface of the protective earth to face the sun. This is where things get *done*, where targets are set and met, where competition is encouraged and victory is celebrated. This is where the project hits the road, is experimented with, put into action. "The Winner takes all" and "Just do it!" sum up this stance. As long as there is a task to be accomplished or a medal to be won, the warriors among us will be striving to achieve them. But this too, is not the end. Eventually our Action will need analysis and Order.

And so we come to the last of the four characters, the Good King, where the masculine and the static energies combine to produce appropriate boundaries. This is where the results of the experiment are carefully weighed before committing to a long-term distribution of the product or project. Here we build structure into a process, formulate strategy and define the rules and regulations. This character wants to understand things, to frame them and categorize them for future reference. They tend to work "by the book" (they will often have written "the book" as well!) They seek out as much information as possible before making a decision and, above all, obey the laws of logic.

The model is fluid and cyclical, so it does not end – when one project is rolled out, another begins, and when a product comes to the natural end of its life the cycle starts again. This can be anything from a simple re-branding exercise (a minor change to enhance vitality), to a death and re-birth (a major shift in identity – like a corporate take-over in which one firm is swallowed by another). Whichever it is, the seed is sown and off we go again.

Until 25 years ago a leader could mostly get away with only playing the masculine characters, planning and action were the order of the day. But that day has passed. The rate of change and the need for relationships has brought the feminine characters into equal prominence for the 21st century leader.

"TYPECASTING"

As human beings we all have one or two favoured characters that we tend to play better than the others. In organizations we often get early recognition for playing these well and are then promoted or moved around because of it: "That team needs a prod into action, send X in to run it, she'll get them moving...", or "This department needs some more creative thinking about the future, Y will give them some new ideas...", etc. Which is fine as long as we are managing a process or running a team. But when we move into higher positions of leadership, when we have to oversee projects from initial vision to final analysis, and lead others whose favourite characters range around the model, then we need to access all four characters.

"INNER RESOURCES"

Each character has certain skills, attitudes and behaviours that are most readily associated with it (see below). This is not an exact science but a generalization. When someone recognizes their particular favourite

Leadership Potential Chart

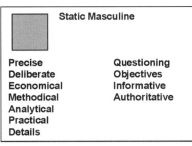

Static Masculine	
Precise	Questioning
Deliberate	Objectives
Economical	Informative
Methodical	Authoritative
Analytical	
Practical	
Details	

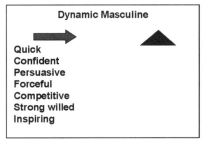

Dynamic Masculine	
Quick	
Confident	
Persuasive	
Forceful	
Competitive	
Strong willed	
Inspiring	

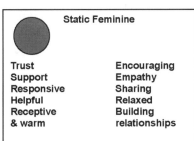

Static Feminine	
Trust	Encouraging
Support	Empathy
Responsive	Sharing
Helpful	Relaxed
Receptive	Building
& warm	relationships

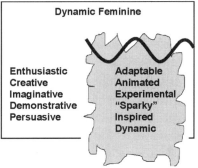

Dynamic Feminine	
Enthusiastic	Adaptable
Creative	Animated
Imaginative	Experimental
Demonstrative	"Sparky"
Persuasive	Inspired
	Dynamic

Henry's Journey

character, people around them at work would generally agree that they exhibit these characteristics, especially when things are going well.

These skills and behaviours are the "inner resources", the "toys we bring to the party", the "youth on fire" to help us achieve the mission at hand. And they are invaluable. They may also be limited – in fact at some point in the project they *will* be limited. If we have not (deliberately or intuitively) learnt how to switch roles when necessary we will come up against a stumbling block. The map of Henry's journey (see above) is differently shaded to highlight the areas of the play where Henry needs to play the different characters. If he were unable to change role he would not achieve his desired goal.

The Medicine Woman allows him access to the imagination and the capacity to vision the future. The Good King teaches him how to assess the past and allocate appropriate resources to achieve the vision. The

56

Warrior gives him the edge needed to deal with the Traitors, make tactical decisions on the battlefield and inspire the troops to fight against overwhelming odds. And without the Great Mother he would never be able to survive the "dark night" – to manage fear and doubt in himself and others, simultaneously and differently – nor would he consider turning the battlefield into a garden when the fighting is over. There are many more specific points in the play when we could see him embodying more of one character then another, but I hope this general overview makes the point. He needs all four.

"INNER TRAITORS" – UNDERPLAYING CHARACTERS

People naturally tend to play their favoured characters more often than the others. We may even try to miss out or skim over the part of a project that requires us to engage with our least favourite character. In extreme cases we may fail to recognize that these parts of a project are necessary at all. If the Medicine Woman is our least favourite character we may squeeze the time we allow for brainstorming and creative thinking before a project begins. If we don't much like the Warrior we may not deal with the external traitors, and so on.

This avoidance can turn into an "inner traitor" that trips us up. If we remain unaware of our tendency to avoid this character it becomes even more dangerous.

One potential "inner traitor" is the tendency to underplay our least favourite character; another comes from overplaying our favourite.

"INNER TRAITORS" – OVERPLAYING CHARACTERS

If we never leave the place occupied by our favourite character, or if we always return to it as soon as possible, we will eventually appear to those around us to turn into the negative version of the positive potential. And if we keep going in this manner long enough we *will* turn into the negative. It is possible to have too much of a good thing!

Becoming negative version of positive potential

So the wonderful sparky, excitable ideas person can have too many ideas for the good of his or her team, department or organization. They may come up with three different versions when one would have been enough. And before one change project has been completed they will start the next and plan a third. Eventually those around them will say "They're insane – this is too much!" The Medicine Woman has become the Mad Woman.

The trustworthy, relationship-focused person may spend too much time looking after others, to the detriment of important organizational goals. I worked with a social services department recently who, when a key member of their team came into work late five days in a row, without explanation, mustered the supreme courage on the fifth day to ask them if they wanted to sit down and have a cup of tea and talk about it – instead of demanding an explanation and better timekeeping. The Great Mother can turn into the Devouring Mother, suffocating or smothering the very potential they are trying to nurture and release.

The aggressive, action-orientated go-getter may never stop. They simply set a new, higher target and want it met quicker than the last one. People walk around them in a state of anxiety, fearing they, like others before them, will become expendable cannon fodder. The habitual fighter forgets to put away the sword and often leaves a trail of bloodshed behind them, even when walking through their own troops! Others will think this type are only interested in furthering their own careers, maximizing their own bonuses. The heroic Warrior can become the Mercenary Tyrant.

The Good King can fall in love with their own structure and refuse to allow any room for change or growth. They want rules and regulations and want them to be obeyed, sometimes even simply because... it says so in the manual (and particularly if they wrote the manual!) They may ring fence their power base and hunker down, refusing entry or help to those younger who may be ambitious. They also tend to avoid risk. If they get overtaken on the career ladder they may turn cynical and resistant. The Good King turns into the Bitter Old Man.

Negative Leadership Potentials

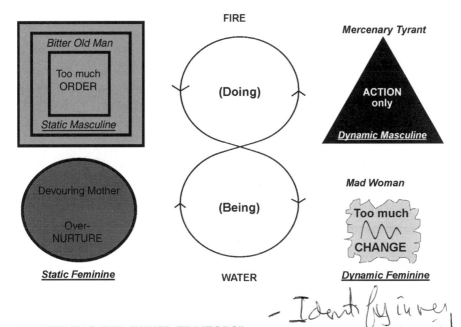

FIRE

Bitter Old Man

Too much
ORDER

Static Masculine

(Doing)

Mercenary Tyrant

ACTION
only

Dynamic Masculine

Devouring Mother

Over-
NURTURE

Static Feminine

(Being)

WATER

Mad Woman

Too much

CHANGE

Dynamic Feminine

— Identify inner
traitors,

IDENTIFYING THE "INNER TRAITORS"

When we work with groups we ask everyone to identify which of these habits is most likely to get in their own way of achieving the project in hand. Which "inner traitor" will stop you getting to France? Is it the underplaying of a least favourite character, or overplaying a favourite, that could trip you up?

I have thought about writing this book for three years and was beginning to wonder why it was not happening. When I looked for potential "inner traitors" the reason became blindingly obvious. My favourite character is the creative Medicine Woman, closely followed by the inspiring Warrior – put them together and I am a fully signed up member of "Dynamics Anonymous". I am happiest creating new workshops, working on new themes, putting the ideas into action and delivering the goods. I am not so good at ordering my time, managing long-term goals and looking after others and myself in the meantime. Which meant, of course, that every time I started to apply myself to the long-term project of writing a book I would get sidetracked by sparkier short-term opportunities that offered more unexpected discoveries than sitting in front of a computer. It was actually during a *Henry V* seminar, when some bright participant asked me, at this point in the proceedings, what exactly were my "inner traitors" that I saw how my failure to play the "Good King" was stopping me writing. Still, at least it was an unexpected discovery, so I couldn't complain!

DIFFERENT "INNER TRAITORS" AT DIFFERENT LEVELS

The characters can also be applied to whole teams, departments, even organizations. When I work in-house some of the key learning comes from sharing opinions as to what the departmental or organizational "inner traitors" might be, and then deciding what to do about them. The desired change almost always requires the department or organization to learn a new character and stop being dominated by an old one.

A chemical company that wanted its people to take pride in their work was dominated by the Warrior ethic in its culture. The old style was very command and control and hierarchical, but now they needed to change character. They simply could not command people to feel better or bully them into enjoying their work. They needed to enter a relationship and listen – in other words, learn to play the Great Mother a bit more and the Warrior a bit less. In the end they decided to consult with a cross section of staff as to what *they* would need in order for the desired change to have a chance of growing into reality – and then ask the staff what the top team could do to help.

The social services department mentioned above required the opposite move. Immersed in the caring and sharing of the Great Mother character, they needed to play the Warrior in order to "motivate the troops", discipline bad practice and make their targets.

KEEPING WATCH

Without awareness there is no chance of change. Without Henry being aware that there will be traitors (both inner and outer) trying to stop him reaching his goal, there would be no chance of catching them in time. Awareness is the beginning of changing the old pattern. Then it takes motivation to follow it through. If our passion to pursue our "France" is greater than the resistance to changing our old ways, we are in with a fighting chance. If not, our project may end up dead in the water. In Act 5 we will explore how we can rehearse these new behaviours and add new characters to our repertoire. It is enough to notice for now that a) we need to and b) it's tough.

The following poem by James Autry relates how hard it is to change from Warrior and Good King and integrate the Great Mother.

RESISTING

- Awareness.

- It's tough

There are days when the old ways seem easier.
To hell with consensus
and community building
and conflict resolution
and gentle persuasion.
Time to kick some ass,
turn some heads around,
get some action,
make this place move.
Time to stop asking questions
and give some orders.
Time to get things
ready for inspection.

It's an old urge,
the luxury of power,
the first temptation of bosshood,
and it comes like a bad temper
on a day when someone won't accept
the answer
I gave,

and pushes again,
another five-minute meeting that eats up an hour,
another printout to prove a point not worth proving,
another ploy to protect someone's invisible turf,
another dance along that border
between debate and defiance.
I feel the anger flashing
and fight what I want to say,
all the top-sergeant stuff
like "Shape up or ship out"
or "Tell it to the chaplain."
When I'm lucky,
the thought of those words
bouncing off the panelled walls
makes me smile.
When I'm not,
I take a very deep breath.

And here we will leave the "inner traitors" – for the moment. It is time to look at what – and who – can get in our way externally.

ACT 2 • Scene 1

Old friends

THE STORY

After the honourable pitch of the Chorus we come down to earth in a tavern. We meet Henry's old mates (from *Henry IV Parts 1* and *2*) Nym, Bardolph, Pistol, Mistress Quickly and a boy. They are involved in petty jealousies and infighting – Pistol apparently having stolen Quickly away from Nym and Nym refusing to pay Pistol a gambling debt. They keep attempting to start a fight and Bardolph keeps intervening until the boy declares their old mentor rogue Falstaff to be "very sick" in bed. This brings them to a truce and an agreed understanding for the first time in the scene when Nym says "The King hath run bad humours on the night; that's the even of it", and Pistol replies "Nym thou hast spoke the right, his heart is fracted and corroborate". They exit with Pistol assuring them "Let us condole the knight, for, lambkins, we will live."

THE SPIN OF HONOUR

The Chorus has been cast as the storyteller – but he does not tell the truth. He is a Renaissance spin-doctor who promises us that "honour's thought reigns solely in the breast of every man." But his noble speech is immediately followed by the tavern dwellers whose sole thoughts are women, fighting and money. Honour could not be further from their hearts or minds if it tried! We only have to glance back at the prequel to see their mentor Falstaff's real thoughts about honour:

> *What is honour? A word. What is in that word honour? Air.*
> *Who hath it? He that died on Wednesday. Doth he feel it? No.*
> *Doth he hear it? No. 'Tis insensible then. Yea, to the dead. But*
> *will it live with the living? No. Therefore I'll none of it.*
>
> (Henry IV Part 1, Act 5 Scene 1)

INCLUSIVITY

I don't believe that Shakespeare is just sending himself up with this deliberate juxtaposition of honourable and dishonourable intentions; he is making a case for human inclusiveness and increased awareness. We will always tend to lead others the way we want to be led, but until we understand what truly motivates others we will be unable to appeal to their followership effectively.

Shakespeare is inclusive in his plays, he does not ostracize those who do not share the leader's point of view (unless they threaten his life) but includes them in his universe – just as the Globe Theatre embraces monarchs and groundlings alike in its circular architecture.

These apparently baser, dishonourable characters add much humour and humanity to the play. They give depth and reality and street smarts. There is a very real way in which they provide the guts of the play, not courage but stomach – appetite.

In the Renaissance philosophy of the time there was a general belief in different levels of existence, different bodies and different elements – of which these characters are an essential part.

THE FOUR ELEMENTS

At the bottom lies the Earth element, the physical body, the level of animal nature and natural appetite. Our friends from the tavern are such figures, always wanting something throughout the play; sex, money, food, drink, etc. In the Globe Theatre this element is represented by the under

Four Levels In The Theatre

stage, the underworld, the pit. At the same level as the under-stage (and nearly the same height) stand the groundlings, the lower class, fun loving, food-throwing part of the audience who won't put up with too much high falluting poetry without a comic turn thrown in now and again.

Next comes the Water element, the emotional body where we are pulled on tides of feeling from one pole to another, from one pillar to another. The law of opposites that is so deftly drawn by Shakespeare in so many of his great plays. The tug between strife and friendship, love and war, justice and mercy, husband and wife, father and son, murderer and victim, etc. Where we feel ourselves shifting allegiance, unsure of our ground, treading the floor of the stage on the ground of life itself.

Then comes the Air element, represented on the stage by the musicians' gallery. This is the place of harmonious and pure thought, the place of Juliet's balcony in *Romeo and Juliet*. This is the abode of those who are not quite embroiled in the ebb and flow of everyday life but have an overview, can see where things should go in order to achieve a more harmonious resolution.

Last but not least is the realm of Fire, the place of inspiration and imagination, represented in the theatre by the "heavens", the gold painted roof above the stage. This is the place from which descend gods and goddesses, that which is beyond daily life or normal comprehension. It is the place appealed to by the first Chorus in our play when he asks for "a muse of fire, that would ascend the brightest heaven of invention".

For Shakespeare, no society is complete that does not include all four levels, all four modes of existence. And all four exist within us as different potentials, different bodies. As the writer Rumer Godden put it: "There is an Indian proverb that says that everyone is in a house with four rooms, a physical, an emotional, a mental and a spiritual. Most of us tend to live in one room most of the time but, unless we go into every room every day, even if only to keep it aired, we are not a complete person".

While many religious traditions urge us to transcend or forego the pleasures and appetites to be found on the physical earthly plane, Shakespeare urges them to be understood, taken into account and included.

NECESSARY SACRIFICE

However, there is a big distinction between including diversity and embracing those who prefer riot and dishonour to making a positive difference. Henry has sacrificed part of the person he used to be as Prince Hal:

> *I have turn'd away my former self,*
> *So will I those that kept me company.*

(Henry IV Part 2, Act 5 Scene 5)

It is a necessary sacrifice if he wishes to be taken seriously as a leader. If he brings Falstaff to a strategy meeting he will be in big trouble. Some people will be waiting for Henry to trip up, to return to his old habits and old friends. He can't afford to give these people the chance *not* to trust him. As an American friend once said to me: "You can't fly like an eagle if you hang out with a bunch of turkeys!"

Many kings and leaders in the past have abused their privileges, engaged in cronyism and promoted their friends (some would say this still happens today!) But such people lose the respect of others and can only attract followers by bribing or bullying. Henry has made the choice to take his leadership role seriously and only surround himself with those who deserve to be there; "limbs of noble counsel, that the great body of our state may go in equal rank with the best governed nation" (*Henry IV Part 2*, Act 5 Scene 2).

Moving into leadership involves a step into authority. If others are truly qualified you can bring them with you. If not, either you move away from them or they move away from you. There is loneliness at the top and an inspirational leader's best friend may often be their vision. This is why Henry is prepared to take hard decisions along the way – because he is not just in it for himself. The "angel of consideration" has broadened his range of concern to include a whole nation. He cannot endanger their interests by involving himself with underworld characters, even though they may have taught him some street smarts along the way. These particular old friends have to be kept at a distance.

OLD HABITS *Old Habits / Old Friends*

We could say the same for some of our appetites and old habits. These "inner old friends" can also lead us to dishonour and disrespect if we're not careful. ("President Clinton, did you ask the witness to lie?" – "No sir, just kneel.") A wise leader will want to understand their own motivation, appetites and habits. What are the appetites in you that might stop you getting to "France"? *Banishing them.*

I have some appetites of my own to confess; television and wine. After a day's work my reflex action (old habit) was to sit down in front of the TV, no matter what was on, drink half a bottle of wine and numb out. But in order to commit to my "France", and sign the contract for this book, I would have to make a sacrifice. I needed that time most evenings for sober thinking and writing. If I simply hung out with the "old friends" I would be seriously impeding the mission. I took advice from a mentor, Robert Bly, who warned me that the psyche likes deals, it doesn't do well with simple banishment orders. In other words, if we simply try to deny an appetite and close a door on it, it will likely come in through a back door and take us by surprise. It is better to negotiate with it in advance and provide for it. Henry does this with his old friends, as his brother John says: "He hath intent his wonted followers shall all be very well provided for" (*Henry IV Part 2*, Act 5 Scene 5).

My deal ended up being a couple of good videos and a good bottle of wine every weekend, in exchange for five weekday evenings to pursue the project in hand. You could say that I banished my "inner old friends" during the week, but provided for them at the weekends.

Henry has banished these particular old tavern friends from within 10 miles of his person. He does not mention Falstaff in our play; it is left to his other mates to bring him to our attention.

What habits do you have that may require a similar court order?

ACT 2 • Scene 2

Managing the "disagreers" (and dealing with the traitors)

THE STORY

Henry's loyal nobles watch the King talking with Cambridge, Grey and Scroop, who have been discovered to be traitors, and wonder at his courage:

EXETER   *Fore God, his grace is bold to trust these traitors.*

GLOUCESTER   *The King hath note of all that they intend,*
                     By interception which they dream not of.

Henry then proceeds slowly and cleverly to wind a net around the traitors. He says he intends to pardon a man who shouted at him in public the previous day. The traitors urge punishment to the full extent of the law, but Henry insists on mercy. He then gives each traitor a document, supposedly royal instructions, but actually an account of their treachery, and remarks; "what see you in those papers, that you lose so much complexion?" They immediately throw themselves upon the King's mercy, but Henry is not in a forgiving vein:

> *The mercy that was quick in us but late*
> *By your own counsel is suppressed and killed.*
> *You must not dare, for shame, to talk of mercy,*
> *For your own reasons turn into your bosoms,*
> *As dogs upon their masters, worrying you.—*
> *See you, my princes and my noble peers,*
> *These English monsters!...*
> *What shall I say to thee, Lord Scroop, thou cruel,*
> *Ingrateful, savage, and inhuman creature?*

Thou that didst bear the key of all my counsels,
That knew'st the very bottom of my soul,
That almost mightst have coined me into gold
Wouldst thou have practised on me for thy use...
                'Tis so strange
That though the truth of it stands off as gross
As black on white, my eye will scarcely see it...
                Thy fall hath left a kind of blot
To mark the full-fraught man, and best endowed,
With some suspicion. I will weep for thee,
For this revolt of thine methinks is like
Another fall of man.

The Duke of Exeter arrests them and the King pronounces sentence:

God 'quit you in his mercy. Hear your sentence.
You have conspired against our royal person,
Joined with an enemy proclaimed,
And from his coffers
Received the golden earnest of our death,
Wherein you would have sold your King to slaughter...
His subjects to oppression and contempt,
And his whole kingdom into desolation.
Touching our person seek we no revenge,
But we our kingdom's safety must so tender,
Whose ruin you have sought, that to her laws
We do deliver you. Get ye therefore hence,
Poor miserable wretches, to your death.

They are taken out while Henry turns to his loyal nobles, seeking to make the most of an unhappy situation:

Now lords for France, the enterprise whereof
Shall be to you, as us, like glorious.

We doubt not of a fair and lucky war,
Since God so graciously hath brought to light
This dangerous treason lurking in our way
To hinder our beginnings. We doubt not now
But every rub is smoothèd on our way...
Cheerly to sea, the signs of war advance:
No King of England, if not King of France.

THE KING'S GIFTS

In *Henry IV Part 1* we saw Henry pretending to be a bandit when he robbed his cronies of their ill gotten gains (see Introduction – The story of Henry's past). Later he engaged in a role-play game with Falstaff, pretending to be his father, the King. In *Henry IV Part 2* he disguised himself as a serving man to Falstaff in the tavern without being recognized. One of the many gifts Henry's past experiences have given him is the ability to play and to act. Sometimes an effective leader needs to be an effective actor. Dealing with potential traitors is one of those times.

He knows who the traitors are and what they intend (to kill him in Southampton), yet he talks to them as if they were loyal subjects. This takes courage and skill. If he were to make a mistake the consequences would be dire. Henry uses himself as bait to ensure that they are caught, and then makes sure they know how he feels about their betrayal. He is determined not to sweep their treachery under the carpet or to deal with it privately. He exposes it publicly and, as a result, sends strong messages to those around; that he will use "transparency" as far as is reasonable, and that he will not tolerate corruption. (As we shall see in Acts 3 and 4, Henry remains consistent to these principles, even in the heat of a campaign.)

POLITICAL INTELLIGENCE

The King hath note of all that they intend,
By interception which they dream not of.

If Henry was not aware there might be traitors around he would not have a chance in hell of catching them. Many managers operate on the naïve principle that if they are honest; everyone else will be too. Wrong. The other nice people will, but the traitors won't. And let's not forget the key difference between a traitor and an enemy: a traitor used to be your friend – and has probably not told you the friendship is over – just like Lord Scroop in the play.

Leaders need to know who will oppose their mission as much as they need to know who will support it. Some "Disagreers" will voice their opposition publicly but many will do it privately. So an effective leader is advised to keep their ear to the ground, and actively consider who might line up in opposition. Who has something to lose if the project goes ahead? Whose territory might be subtly invaded or their authority eroded?, etc. When we raise our flag to declare our mission we will certainly attract Providence and supporters who otherwise would not realize what we want to do. We will also attract detractors, those who wish to shoot down our project, and those who want to depose us as leaders.

Such folk exist in every major organization; it comes with the territory. If there is power, money or prestige up for grabs, there will be several people willing to make a grab, and they may not tell you who they are. Many potential saboteurs justify their actions with the belief that things would be better if they were in charge and therefore it is in the common interest to betray you. Having worked across all sectors I can assure you that this is not sector specific. The organization I know which had the greatest numbers of traitors per capita was a Church charity. The message is simple. Watch your back.

The aim here is to raise awareness not to promote paranoia. If you have invested in a vision and built consent around a mission, it makes sense to protect it, and you, from treacherous attack. It is in the interests of those around you as well.

THE THREE TYPES OF "DISAGREERS"

We only see Henry dealing with the traitors in the play. But, of course, not everyone who disagrees with us is a traitor (even though it sometimes feels that way). During seminars we have identified three different types of "Disagreers": the Naysayers, the Critics and the Traitors. These are the people who will, overtly or covertly, disagree with a leader and/or their "France".

The Naysayer is not afraid to say no. They are the opposite of the "Yeasayer", who agrees with everything the leader says. The Naysayer is up front and honest about their disagreements. They often have another idea, want to get their point across and can cause trouble if they are not listened to.

The Critics are those people who just seem to prefer criticizing to doing anything else. They tend to negate every new idea and look for the problems first. The French writer Henry David Thoreau had a wonderful phrase: "It is better to light a candle than to curse the darkness". The Critics prefer to curse the darkness, and if they can't find any darkness around to curse, they'll have a good go at your candle. Critics may be overt and upfront with their criticisms or they may operate primarily behind your back. However they express their reticence, they will ultimately need to be handled very differently from the Naysayers (more of this later).

And last, but certainly not least, we have the Traitors. These are the people in organizations who, for whatever reason, conscious or unconscious, seek to undermine and sabotage you, your leadership and/or the project you are leading. They either do not want you to hold your current position, or they do not want the current project to happen. Either way, they are very, very dangerous.

Correctly identifying the different types takes time. It involves reading energy, using intuition and piecing together clues. You will never spot the differences by reading intranet memos or e-mails. You will do it through raising your awareness.

DISTINGUISHING NAYSAYERS AND CRITICS

The Naysayers tend to operate with what I call "front foot energy"; the Critics with "back foot energy". The metaphor is drawn from boxing where it is easy to spot those who prefer to move forward and assert themselves in a fight and those who tend to wait, move back and pick their time to counter.

The Naysayer usually wants the organization to move forward, but is disagreeing with the particular way currently being considered. They want movement but not this movement, or at least not now. Their body language moves forward and their gestures are direct.

The Critic tends not to want much movement at all. Energy is invested in holding on to what currently exists, and sometimes the "back foot" manifests as having a foot in the past – bemoaning the loss of some golden age "when things were better... when we knew what was what... when there was less pressure...", etc. Body language is leaning back, backing off, withdrawing physically from the "engagement zone". Gestures tend to be across the body, sideways, waving or batting new ideas away.

There is usually a different tone of voice too. The Naysayer speaks with energy, often from the front of the mouth, uses upbeat vocal tones and often ends sentences on an upward inflection. The Critic typically speaks with low energy, the voice comes from the back of the throat, using withdrawn downbeat tones and often ending with a downward inflection.

If you really listen to someone talking in a meeting and observe their body language it becomes apparent if they are more front foot or back foot. As always, we have to be careful about jumping to quick assumptions. Mr X may sound deflated because of an illness in the family, Mrs Y may be leaning back and appear bored because of a migraine. But if we keep looking and listening over a period of time we can build up a picture of a pattern of behaviour. We may also want to check out our assumptions with trusted others: "Do you get the sense that Z is not really with us on this...?"

It takes a little of the Great Mother skills to raise awareness in this way. The Warrior may never look beyond the projected targets to the human faces across the table.

DISTINGUISHING CRITICS AND TRAITORS

There are two different types of Critics; Overt and Covert. The Overt Critics speak up in public; Covert Critics speak critically only in private, around corridors, in the canteen or the pub – anywhere that is safely behind the leader's back.

This is why Covert Critics and Traitors are the most difficult to distinguish. A clever traitor will also rarely, if ever, criticize in public; they bide their time and turn others against you in private.

So the main difference between a Covert Critic and a Traitor is their intended result. The Critic intends things to stay as they are, to protect their turf, to avoid change. The Traitor seeks a change of leader or the end of a particular project. They seek a negative change for you.

You probably sense a 2 × 2 model coming on, so here it is.

Distinguishing The Disagreers

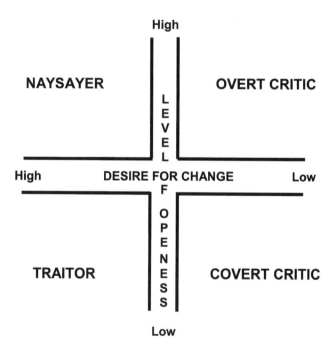

When faced with a Disagreer, can you identify their level of openness and their general desire for change?

It is best to start identifying potential supporters and detractors early on. Start the distinguishing process between the Naysayers and the Critics and then see who's left. Who is it that appears to be on board, is not acting openly against the project but whom logic or past experience dictates would not normally be for it? Have they changed or might they be hiding their disagreement and looking for an opening to bring the project down?

JEALOUSY OR ENVY?

Another energetic distinction between the types is one between what I call "Jealousy" and "Envy". Let us say that jealousy is what happens when I look at someone who has something I want: a job, access to a budget, the ear of a big boss or whatever. That feeling motivates me to get it for myself. So I might go on an extra training programme, put in that extra couple of hours a week, go for a drink on Friday with those people, even join that golf club, etc. The jealous impulse can cause me to raise myself up to the level of the object of jealousy.

Envy, in this scheme, is a more negative impulse, when I look at someone who has something I want, and I don't want them to have it. So I try to bring them down rather than raise myself up. In cases of extreme envy people will bring down whole projects (sometimes whole organizations) as long as the object of envy is brought down too.

The Naysayers and the Overt Critics tend to be jealous, the Covert Critics and the Traitors envious.

Another colleague (let's call him A), working in the civil service some years ago, was assigned to produce a training plan for a new equal opportunities policy. He zealously pursued his task, researching possibilities and combining it with a plan to introduce a whole new management style into the organization. His peer (B) was actually responsible for implementing the policy but was bitterly opposed to it, finding one excuse after another to stall the process. When a letter was received by the Chief Executive (C) querying progress from above, it was sent on to B who reported that progress had not been possible because A had failed in his duty to produce a training plan. Luckily C thought this failure of duty unlike A, and called him in to talk about it personally. Only then did it become clear that treachery was afoot. Not only had B acted to subvert the policy, but his envy of A's ability to innovate had led him to try to destroy A rather than harness his ideas for the good of the organization.

TRICKING THE TRICKSTERS

So... how do you spot a Traitor before it is too late? The play does not shed much light on this. The Chorus introduces us to the traitors Cambridge, Grey and Scroop (Henry knows who they are before this scene begins). Since they have not revealed themselves it is fair to assume that Henry has used espionage to identify them. He is also prepared to use trickery to get the desired result. Henry consults them about forgiving a man who railed at him the previous day (a minor misdemeanour compared with conspiracy to kill a king) and the traitors – anxious no doubt to appear evangelically supportive of Henry in public – advise severe punishment. When their treachery is revealed they plead for mercy; to which Henry is able to reply:

> *The mercy that was quick in us but late*
> *By your own counsel is suppressed and killed.*
> *You must not dare, for shame, to talk of mercy,*
> *For your own reasons turn into your bosoms,*
> *As dogs upon their masters, worrying you.*

The words "your own petard" and "hoist with" spring to mind. This ability to turn the tables against the unscrupulous is an essential survival skill. In mythology there is an oft-repeated motif in which a young hero or heroine has to outwit thieves and set a trap to rob the robbers. And this, we may remember, is precisely what Henry has learnt to do in the tavern.

Some managers ask: "How can you talk about service and ethics in Henry's leadership and then support him spying on people and tricking them?" I usually respond: "Would you rather he remained an innocent, virtuous leader who died of a mysterious knife wound at Southampton?" If you are inspired enough to come up with a project that has the potential to make a positive difference, it behoves you to be sly enough to remain alive to complete it.

In some cultures this particular ability is deliberately taught to the young. Guatemalan shaman Martín Prechtel relates how youth in the Mayan tradition are taken away from their homes to be initiated into the responsibilities of adulthood and are set trials and ordeals to overcome. One of the first of these is to return to the hut of their mother without being seen and steal her huge family cooking pot. Except, of course, the mothers know the youths are coming and wait with sticks to beat them away. The youths often end up putting the pot over their heads and crouching low so the sticks cannot reach them as they run off, pleased with their success. Until, that is, they learn of their next task, which is to return the pot, without being seen, while Mother waits with stick. (Some chairmen apparently feel this way about shareholder meetings.)

IDENTIFYING THE TRAITORS

How might we trick Traitors into revealing themselves? How can we turn the tables? A word of warning, this is not an exact science, we are trying to read clues left by those who deliberately cover their tracks. It is not straightforward and there may be times when the behaviours mentioned below have innocent motives.

Also, we don't want to get paranoid and think everyone is out to get us (unless they are!). There will almost always be trusted supporters around who can help by keeping their ears to the ground. Sometimes they try to protect us from the canteen gossip by not revealing what they know, so we should make the invitation clear; "I need your help" usually does it.

So, if at some time one of your friends walks up to a group after a meeting and they instantly stop talking, that could be a clue. What is it that they were talking about that your friend is not allowed to overhear? Be aware of eye contact; eyes in a group often flick to the ringleader to check out a reaction. And will do so again if a sticky issue comes up, or a subject that has been under covert discussion. It is hard to fake "welcome" in the eyes – the lips may smile, we are used to making them respond socially, but the eyes show genuine feeling. It is not for nothing we call them "the windows of the soul".

Although many of us are able to disguise some of our feelings some of the time, there are very few who can disguise strong feelings all of the time. All Traitors have strong feelings opposing you or your project, and it is that depth of feeling that may just give them away. Consequently, we look for a discrepancy between what is said and what is really being felt.

The body finds it harder to lie than the mind. If someone comes up to us and speaks about something we despise, and we are not in a position to tell them so, our body instinctively tries to put distance between us and the person speaking. We edge away. Therefore it is possible to observe certain people when we talk to them about the project in hand. If they are on board they tend to lean in or move slightly towards you – engaging with your physical space – and thereby revealing their support for or interest in the subject under discussion. They may stay still, which is a non-committal response, or they may lean back or edge subtly away, suggesting a lack of support for or interest in the subject.

Try out the following. Hand a potential Traitor an important piece of paper connected with a project you are leading and watch what happens. The quicker the paper is removed from their eye line the more they are likely to hold some unspoken resistance to what the paper represents. Again, imagine someone gave you a piece of paper representing some hated project, how would you react? You would probably not want to look at it for long. Nor do they.

Because they have rejected the leader/project internally, and can't afford to do so externally, we have to watch for the moments when the internal reveals itself in the external; in the body, gesture, eye contact and voice.

If having run some of these strategies you still feel you need more evidence, set up a situation where they will have to support publicly the project. Remember the visible commitment at the end of Act 1? This is the one thing Traitors cannot do. Ask them to explain the project to another group or department on your behalf, then ask them to show you how they intend to do it. And watch them carefully. Are they committed? Do they believe in what they are saying enough to convince you of their conviction?

(Of course, many people at work have to move forward with projects they may not be completely committed to, and I am not saying a lack of total conviction is a sign of imminent treachery. In this circumstance you are trying to flush out a doubt or disagreement that has not been openly revealed. There is a difference between commitment and slight doubt, and there is an equal difference between slight doubt and hidden animosity. If they are not expressing the doubt to you, why not?)

If they don't reveal the doubt but are obviously unable physically to commit to the project you have another piece of evidence.

Another test is to actually let them loose on such a presentation (a damage limitable one of course, the Board is probably not a good idea) and send a trusted colleague to keep an eye on them. Unless they are a seriously good actor it will be impossible for them to fake enthusiasm for a project they wish to sink. It is even against their self-interest to present well, because if they could deliver with conviction they might convince others it is the right way to go. They will almost inevitably betray the fact that they are sitting outside the project, looking in with a cynical eye, rather than inside the project looking out with belief. Unconsciously they create a distance between themselves and the project under discussion.

When you have identified someone as being a Traitor – be careful. Identification is only the first step. Then you have to deal with them. But just as identifying the Disagreers is a tricky task, so is managing them.

MANAGING THE NAYSAYERS

The first step with all the Disagreers is to listen – at least to those who are willing to talk. Sometimes the Disagreers are right and unless you listen attentively you will never know. If they (and others around them) know that they are right, and that you have ignored them, you will be heading for trouble.

Managed correctly a Naysayer can become one of your most valuable human assets. They are the best bullshit detectors around, and they will keep your feet on the ground. Most leaders have a few "Yeasayers" around, those who think our ideas are wonderful and don't criticize a thing we do or say, ever. They listen to us; all we hear from them is approval. Nice, but unchallenging. (As a young assistant film director I once worked with an old hand who needed someone to shoot second unit film on location. When I put myself forward he said: "Good heavens no. You agree with everything I say. It would be much too uninteresting." Unfortunately he had a point.)

So the Naysayers will keep us on our toes, they will see the realistic objections to our proposals and bring these forward – sometimes, annoyingly enough, before we have thought of them ourselves. If they sense that we will not listen or treat their objections with respect we can turn them into Overt, then Covert Critics and, in the worst case, a potential Traitor who no longer believes we have the capability to lead successfully.

Obviously, it is in our best interest to intervene and take avoiding action before this happens. The advantage of dealing with a Naysayer lies in their openness. They are prepared to be honest with you and you will almost always benefit by reciprocating in kind. Approach them at a convenient time (usually best in private) and tell them what is so; "I wanted to have a word with you. I have listened to what you have been saying in the meetings and I have done my best to take it into account. However, at this time I believe we are going to have to push on with the original plan. I know you disagree with some of it but I'd like to know if you feel able to support the project as a whole and come on board."

Usually the Naysayer on the receiving end of this approach will feel listened to, respected and wanted. From this position they will tell you a straight yes or no. "Thanks for that, yes I have had my objections, but basically I am behind the project." Or, alternatively, "Thanks, but my objections are fairly fundamental, and I believe I'd be better off putting my energy into something I can really get behind." Either way you get clarification and a straight answer.

SILENCING THE CRITICS

The Critic, on the other hand, often needs the equivalent of a wake up call. Or a shut up call. Again, this is better done one to one, unless you are sure the rest of the team is in agreement. (Calling on one member of a team in public can have a scapegoat effect, where everyone smells a bit of blood and wades in as well. Alternatively, and more dangerously for you, they all come to the Critic's aid and you get recast as the unfair bully who can't take negative comment.)

Eventually, however, once you have identified the Critic and they have had their say, it is in your interest to ignore them and silence them. Ignore them because if you keep listening to their complaints they will wear down the energy you need to make things happen. And silence them because they will drain the motivation of others. Sometimes a simple "shut up" will do, as in: "Please keep quiet a moment and listen. I've sat in meetings and heard you complain about this for months. It's not helping. We've all got a job to do here and I need you to stop complaining and get on and do it. And if you can't then I'll find you something else to do somewhere else." It's like a minor turning of the tables – criticizing the Critic. But it often works. Sometimes they even feign ignorance ("Who me? Negative? Surely not!"), but they will be more conscious of their behaviour in the future. They know you have spotted them and you are not going to put up with it any more. (With the Covert Critic you need to amass enough evidence and hearsay from others to be able to stand the same ground.)

If we, as individuals, do not have the credibility/authority/position to get away with it on our own, then ask for help from above. Once your mission has been approved it is in everyone's interest that the Critics don't slow things up and de-motivate the troops. And one thing that worries the inveterate Critic is disapproval from the top. Finally, if all else fails, I suggest you read the following at your next team meeting:

ANSWERING THE CRITIC

It is not the critic who counts; not those
who point out where our strong
people stumbled or when the doer of
deeds could have done better.

The credit belongs to those who are
actually in the arena. Whose faces are
marred by dust and sweat and blood;
who strive valiantly, who err and
come short again and again; who
know great enthusiasms; who at best
know the triumph of high
achievement; and who at worst if they
fall, at least fall while daring greatly.

So that their place will never be with
those cold and timid souls, who know
neither victory nor defeat.

(Anonymous)

Recognize that what sustains the Critic is the fear of failure. They don't want you to fly with an exciting new idea because if it fails they will seem guilty by association. They would rather stand still, be timid, and curse your candle. Our job, as leaders, is not to let them rob us and others of our chance to know the triumph of high achievement.

DEALING WITH TRAITORS

Henry makes an important separation between his human feelings of betrayal and his duty to protect the nation. First he expresses his emotional reaction:

> *What shall I say to thee, Lord Scroop, thou cruel,*
> *Ingrateful, savage, and inhuman creature?...*
> *Wouldst thou have practised on me for thy use...*
> > *'Tis so strange*
> *That though the truth of it stands off as gross*
> *As black on white, my eye will scarcely see it...*
> *O how hast thou with jealousy infected*
> *The sweetness of affiance. Show men dutiful?*
> *Why so didst thou. Seem they grave and learned?*
> *Why so didst thou...*
> *Such, and so finely bolted, didst thou seem.*
> *And thus thy fall hath left a kind of blot*
> *To mark the full-fraught man, and best endowed,*
> *With some suspicion. I will weep for thee,*
> *For this revolt of thine methinks is like*
> *Another fall of man.*

Henry releases his pent up emotion and clears it from his system, before he gives a sober judgement.

People often withhold their emotional response to a betrayal, but then it can sneak up on us in a revenge fantasy.

One executive we worked with arrived in this condition, furious that a peer partner had gone over her head to assign the next year's four promotions to partner level, the responsibility for which was actually hers. Feeling betrayed she, too, had gone upwards and demanded that the promotions be withdrawn, even though she actually agreed with two of them. These deserving workers were in danger of being held back because of her unexpressed anger at the betrayal that was manifesting itself as a desire for revenge. A leader who attempts to judge an apparently treacherous act without expressing the emotional reaction may be perceived as punishing and can lose the respect of others whose trust they require.

The ability to express emotion appropriately, and separate feeling from responsibility, is part of what is now called "emotional intelligence". Some leaders might simply turn around and say "You're fired" and remain seething with anger. Others internalize the betrayal and choose not to trust again. As Henry says, it is all too easy to let one man's fall mark the "full-fraught" (ie honourable) others "with some suspicion".

Having expressed himself as a human, he is then able to judge as a king:

> Hear your sentence.
> You have conspired against our royal person,
> Joined with an enemy proclaimed...
> Wherein you would have sold your King to slaughter,
> His princes and his peers to servitude,
> His subjects to oppression and contempt,
> And his whole kingdom into desolation.
> Touching our person seek we no revenge,
> But we our kingdom's safety must so tender,
> Whose ruin you have sought, that to her laws
> We do deliver you. Get ye therefore hence,
> Poor miserable wretches, to your death.

Henry is quite prepared to be ruthless in the pursuit of his vision, even though it means sentencing an old friend to death. Dealing with Traitors requires Warrior energy. The Great Mother leaders among us often try and turn Traitors into friends, which is a bit like painting a target on your back and saying "Aim here". The fact is that when you identify a Traitor you or they must move on or out. Staying in proximity for anything more than the short term is dangerous to your health.

Fortunately or unfortunately, depending on your point of view, we no longer have the Tower of London waiting to accommodate Traitors.

Dealing with them nowadays is an extremely delicate matter; constructive dismissal suits can start flying if you move them out insensitively.

If they are out to get you and you know it, it is safer to prevent their attack (like Henry) than wait for it (like Julius Caesar). If you have the authority to move them on or out, use it (with discretion); if not, you may again need help from above. This too must be handled prudently because a) the Traitor may have got there first and complained about you and b) unless the request is clearly and demonstrably for the good of the whole it may be perceived as a conflict of personalities which you are unable to handle. If it is not possible for the Traitor to be moved it is worth considering a voluntary move yourself.

> In the civil service example quoted earlier, A did just that; he was seconded out of the organization with the agreement of the Chief Executive for six months. During that time the machinations of the traitor B became apparent to others. He brought about his own downfall and quit a few months later. Only after he had gone did A transfer back. He says that the secondment not only relieved the unbearable tension of being close to someone who sought to undermine him, it gave him time to focus on what was truly important to him at work. It was a blessing in disguise.

Lastly, if all else fails, consider promoting the Traitor. Ouch! This is the hardest option for those with a strong sense of justice. But the types who can turn into Traitors are often those who possess enough drive and ambition to get things done. They may just be stuck in an envious personality conflict with you. If they really want their own budget or department to lead, sometimes the best thing you can do for the organization is to help them. At least they are out of your hair. As they say in the armed forces: "Give me a trouble-making private, and I'll make him a sergeant."

HAPPY ENDINGS

Now lords for France, the enterprise whereof
Shall be to you, as us, like glorious.

Henry always attempts to turn situations to his advantage and to paint them in the best light when he speaks to others. He could look at the traitors either way. The fact that they were there at all could have been a bad omen, a dark cloud overshadowing the expedition. Think of a big project you are involved with. How would you feel it if was revealed that the Finance Director (Scroop was Henry's Treasurer) and two other senior managers had been plotting your downfall? But Henry resolutely holds the incident up to the light as good fortune:

> *We doubt not of a fair and lucky war,*
> *Since God so graciously hath brought to light*
> *This dangerous treason lurking in our way*
> *To hinder our beginnings.*

He refuses to be brought down physically or emotionally by the traitors or to let his team dwell on the negative. He refocuses minds on the task at hand:

> *Dear countrymen,*
> *Cheerly to sea, the signs of war advance:*
> *No King of England, if not King of France.*

ACT 2 • Scene 3

An old friend dies

THE STORY

We meet the folk from the tavern on the road to Southampton to join the French expedition. We hear from Pistol that: "Falstaff he is dead".

They are depressed and share stories about their erstwhile leader. Mistress Quickly gives a moving description of his death and says: "The

King hath killed his heart". Pistol, the new head honcho, tries to cheer them up:

> *Yokefellows in arms,*
> *Let us to France, like horseleeches, my boys,*
> *To suck, to suck, the very blood to suck!*

THE KING'S RESPONSIBILITY

Falstaff is dead. Is it Henry's fault?

One would probably have to include Falstaff's lifetime of drunken debauchery in the equation somewhere, as he says: "A pox of this gout, or a gout of this pox! For the one or the other plays the rogue with my great toe" (*Henry IV Part 2*, Act 1 Scene 2). But the sudden and public termination of an important friendship, and the end of his expectation of attaining high office, could not have helped. The country's gain – a responsible king – was undoubtedly Falstaff's loss, and it proved a loss he never recovered from.

I once came across an organizational example that had uncanny parallels to this dilemma. Jan came to a seminar in a "dark night of the soul" situation, looking for a way forward. He was a senior executive from the English headquarters of a European media company, and had been recruited by Pierre, who became a good friend and mentor to him, helping Jan up the ranks. Pierre was by all accounts a Falstaffian figure; the life and soul of the office, a heavy drinker and the centre of fun around which social life revolved. But as the years rolled by Pierre remained more interested in extended lunches than in developing the business. He could rarely work in the afternoons. He was naturally passed over for promotion and warned several times about the effects of his behaviour. Eventually Jan, too, was promoted over Pierre – who became his direct report. Jan was told by his CEO that Pierre's drink problem was becoming an embarrassment to the company. Either Jan would persuade Pierre to get treatment and sober up, or he would have to fire him.

Jan dreaded this task, but he did his best, talking with his old mentor over the course of a whole year about the necessity for him to get his act together. Pierre always promised he would, next week. Eventually it became clear that next week would never come, and Jan was put in the position of having to issue legal warnings, and when these were also breached, firing his old friend. A month later Pierre committed suicide. Now Jan felt responsible and was on the verge of quitting.

Was it his fault? I don't think so, and nor did the other participants in what was becoming by that time a rather heavy seminar room. He was exercising the hard responsibilities of leadership. If the company allowed the behaviour to continue it would have sent out a message that it was OK to have three-hour lunches and come back drunk. The business as a whole would have lost respect and probably contracts too. Jan did not have a choice. The outcome was tragic, but not foreseeable. Jan had certainly never intended the negative outcome that was the unfortunate result. If he now quit as a result, the company would have lost two people as a result of one man's addiction.

We talked through Henry's treatment of Falstaff at some length and role played his last meeting with his friend until Jan realized that, at the time he made the decision, there was no other course of action open to him. By the end of the seminar he felt ready to leave this horrible outcome in the past and carry on doing the work he was passionate about. After all, apart from anything else, it is what his friend would have wanted.

Some people become so driven by appetites that no reason can sway them from following their predilection. Our Earthy friends from the tavern will prove to be similarly intractable in their old habits. Even now, they do not go to France to serve Henry or their country, but only to help themselves:

> *Let us to France, like horseleeches, my boys,*
> *To suck, to suck, the very blood to suck!*

ACT 2 • Scene 4

The rival prince

THE STORY

We meet the French Court of King Charles for the first time. The King is concerned about a possible English invasion; his son, the Dauphin, is not however:

> *England... is so idly kinged,*
> *Her sceptre so fantastically borne*
> *By a vain, giddy, shallow, humorous youth,*
> *That fear attends her not.*

The Duke of Exeter arrives with a message from Henry and hands over the research on law and family lineage prepared by the Archbishop of Canterbury:

> *He sends you this most memorable line,*
> *And... he bids you then resign*
> *Your crown and kingdom, indirectly held*
> *From him, the native and true challenger.*
> KING CHARLES *Or else what follows?*
> EXETER *Bloody constraint. For if you hide the crown*
> *Even in your hearts, there will he rake for it.*
> *If requiring fail, he will compel...*
> *This is his claim, his threat'ning, and my message—*

He then tells the Dauphin that Henry intends to call him to a "hot answer" for the "bitter mock" of the tennis balls. The Dauphin replies that he is willing to fight any king so full of "youth and vanity". Exeter warns him:

You'll find a diff'rence,
Between the promise of his greener days
And these he masters now: now he weighs time
Even to the utmost grain.

The King of France asks for time to consider Henry's proposals.

COMMENT

The Dauphin has a fixed opinion of his challenger which will prove his undoing. He does not consider the possibility that Henry might have changed or developed himself since the first negative reports of his youth. The word "respect" comes from the Latin "re–spectare"; to look again, to look a second time. Leaders need to respect others, particularly the competition, and be flexible in their opinions of others. It is easy to put people into a pigeon hole after one meeting or a couple of negative reports; it is harder to keep an open mind and be prepared to "look again".

Henry has made flexibility an art. He can shape-shift from one character to another with more ease than his rival. He "weighs time" carefully and presents Charles with a well documented, logical case for his claim. Good King strategy. But if his claim is denied he will not go back to the research library. He will shift into Warrior mode: "If requiring fail, he will compel (with) bloody constraint." This ability to balance reason and swiftness, order and action will serve him well.

Act 3

Into battle; first footholds, first setbacks

Photo: John Tramper

Left to right: Nym (Bill Stewart) and Pistol (John McEnery).

Three months into the campaign Henry's army has still not achieved their first objective, taking the town of Harfleur. Henry motivates his troops:

> *Once more unto the breach, dear friends, once more,*
> *Or close the wall up with our English dead.*
> *In peace there's nothing so becomes a man*
> *As modest stillness and humility,*
> *But when the blast of war blows in our ears,*
> *Then imitate the action of the tiger...*
> *Now set the teeth and stretch the nostril wide,*
> *Hold hard the breath, and bend up every spirit*
> *To his full height. On, on, you noblest English...*
> > *The game's afoot.*
> *Follow your spirit, and upon this charge*
> *Cry, "God for Harry! England and Saint George!"*

But he can't motivate everyone alike. His old friends from the tavern are not there for honour, as Nym says:

> *Pray thee corporal, stay. The knocks are too hot,*
> *and for mine own part I have not a case of lives!*

ACT 3 • Chorus

First steps

THE STORY

CHORUS *Suppose that you have seen*
The well-appointed King at Dover pier
Embark his brave fleet,
Holding due course to Harfleur. Follow, follow!
Grapple your minds to sternage of this navy,
And leave your England, as dead midnight still,
Guarded with grandsires, babies, and old women,
For who is he, whose chin is but enriched
With one appearing hair, that will not follow
These culled and choice-drawn cavaliers to France?
Work, work your thoughts, and therein see a siege.
Behold the ordnance on their carriages,
With fatal mouths gaping on girded Harfleur.

THE STORYTELLER'S LICENCE

Once more the Chorus is "economical with the truth". At the end of Act 1 Henry had agreed with Canterbury's proposal that 25% of available troops would go to France while 75% remain to defend England's often-fragile borders with Scotland and Wales. A far cry from the nation peopled only with "grandsires, babies, and old women" suggested by our storyteller. So what is going on?

I believe it is a "dramatic truth" that is being conveyed, not a literal one. Perhaps there is a purpose (maybe even a need) for a leader to have such a storyteller at their disposal. Someone outside of the boardroom who can act as a cheerleader to keep the momentum going, to bolster up the sense that "everyone wants a piece of this one, folks!" The audience in the theatre wants to believe in the "dramatic truth" conveyed by the Chorus, and so do the troops on board the ships bound for France. This sense of pride and honourable intent keep spirits up.

We have probably all known a few of these Storytellers in our time. They may not be the leader of your highest performing team but everyone likes them and listens to them. They tend to inhabit the Medicine Woman and Great Mother characters; they spin great yarns and have a knack of making people feel good.

FIRST STEPS – OUTER

We learn from the Chorus that the first step has been taken. The town of Harfleur has been selected, the ships have set sail, crossed the channel, and the siege has begun.

Often at the beginning of a large enterprise there is no obvious first step. Henry had a whole coastline to choose from. Sometimes the most important thing is simply to decide on a first move, then take it. As we shall see in the next scene, it takes Henry a lot longer than planned to get beyond this first foothold. Looking back no one could really say if it was the right or wrong move. It was the initial action in a campaign that was, eventually, successful. That is what people remember.

Again, it is a balance of the Warrior and Good King energies that operate here. Assess the options, take a decision and move into action.

FIRST STEPS – INNER

Preparation for action happens both externally and internally. I often use a simple Behavioural Action Plan to identify and commit to appropriate inner first steps. Bearing in mind the mission defined in Act 1, and the inner traitors and old appetites named in Act 2, what needs to be done differently in order to move into action at the start of Act 3? With your own mission, what is it that you are currently doing that you will need to *stop* or do *less* of? What is it that you are *not* currently doing that you will need to *start* or do *more* of?

I generally find that people in organizational life are pretty good at starting new things and doing more than they used to – the difficult decision is what to *stop* doing in order to make space for the new. Sometimes it is the apparently small commitments and minor behavioural changes that lead to big differences in the long term. People often find that the Behavioural Stops and Starts are opposite ends of the spectrum, they almost all relate to their favourite and least favourite characters. Here are some recent examples:

WARRIORS
Co-managing Partner, Law firm: *"Stop bullying those around me. Start building relationships for their own sake"*. (Great Mother)

Manager, City trading floor: *"Stop focusing just on short term. Start planning for the future and spending more time with family"*. (Good King and Great Mother)

TV Series Producer: *"Stop competing with members of my own team. Start networking and sharing ideas"*. (Medicine Woman)

GOOD KINGS
Chemical Plant Manager: *"Stop focusing on detail. Start sensing what is important to others"*. (Great Mother)

MD, Engineering company: *"Stop keeping everyone on a short leash. Start trusting others to do the work they were hired to do"*. (Great Mother)

Director, Cabinet Office: *"Stop wanting all the answers before I make a decision. Start allowing room for creative thinking"*. (Medicine Woman)

MEDICINE WOMEN
MD, E-business start up: *"Stop 'fizzing' – coming up with more ideas than staff and capacity can handle. Start consolidating our position"*. (Good King)

Manager, Telecom company: *"Stop using too much time brainstorming in weekly meetings. Start taking on board others' real concerns"*. (Great Mother)

HR Director, Advertising agency: *"Stop getting bored with routine. Start setting simple targets"*. (Warrior)

GREAT MOTHER

Manager, Social services: *"Stop letting staff get away with bad timekeeping. Start motivating the 'troops'"*. (Warrior)

Partner, Accounting firm: *"Stop worrying about what others think. Start setting my own agenda"*. (Good King)

HR Director, Bank: *"Stop looking after everyone, all the time. Start delegating and shut my 'open door' one hour a day"*. (Good King and Warrior)

When I work in-house, particularly with management teams, we spend a long session translating the behaviours they wish to change in their culture into actions that they can physically measure. Just as Henry will know when he has taken Harfleur, we need to know when our first steps have been accomplished.

ACT 3 • Scene 1

Motivating the troops

THE STORY

King Henry enters and speaks to his massed troops:

> *Once more unto the breach, dear friends, once more,*
> *Or close the wall up with our English dead.*
> *In peace there's nothing so becomes a man*
> *As modest stillness and humility,*
> *But when the blast of war blows in our ears,*

Then imitate the action of the tiger.
Stiffen the sinews, conjure up the blood,
Disguise fair nature with hard-favoured rage.
Then lend the eye a terrible aspect,
Let it pry through the portage of the head
Like the brass cannon...
Now set the teeth and stretch the nostril wide,
Hold hard the breath, and bend up every spirit
To his full height. On, on, you noblest English,
Whose blood is fet from fathers of war-proof,
Fathers that like so many Alexanders
Have in these parts from morn till even fought,
And sheathed their swords for lack of argument.
Dishonour not your mothers; now attest
That those whom you called fathers did beget you...
           And you, good yeomen,
Whose limbs were made in England, show us here
The mettle of your pasture; let us swear
That you are worth your breeding—which I doubt not,
For there is none of you so mean and base
That hath not noble lustre in your eyes.
I see you stand like greyhounds in the slips,
Straining upon the start. The game's afoot.
Follow your spirit, and upon this charge
Cry, "God for Harry! England and Saint George!"

FIRST STEPS – FIRST BLOCKS

That's the whole scene. One speech. It could easily be taken as a stirring beginning to the conflict. The only clue that this is not so is that little word "more"; "Once *more* unto the breach..."

Henry has started out with a very reasonable strategy; land at Harfleur in August with 10,000 troops, take it in a week, push on through France and take Paris by Christmas. Sounds sensible enough; except that, like many big projects, things don't quite work out the way they were planned at Head Office. The fact is that at the beginning of Act 3 Scene 1 Henry and his troops have been outside Harfleur for three months, during which time they have lost 2,000 troops. Another 3,000 are ill, and the remaining 5,000, as you might imagine, are not keen to head back into *"that* breach".

COMMON MISTAKES

Now Henry needs to motivate the demoralized troops. There are several key features to the speech, many of which elude modern managers. In workshops we often give people the opportunity to role play motivating their "troops" out of their first blocks. If I were to paraphrase a typical first response to this challenge, it would sound something like the following: "Right you lot. Thanks for coming to the meeting, although I am sure you all know why it has been necessary to call it. I gave you a target when we started; to take this town in a week. It is now three months, *three months* later, and you have still not achieved it. You are way behind schedule and severely over budget. What's more, I am sure it has not escaped your notice that 20% of you are dead, and another 30% have called in sick. What the hell is going on?"

At which point the "troops" are about as keen to fight as they would be to jump off a cliff. All the speaker has done is remind the listeners what has gone wrong. Henry's troops have been living in a marsh for three months, watching their mates die, believe me they *know* what is wrong. What they need is something that can change their energy and create a different result.

The first thing Henry does is to include himself in the conversation: "Once more unto the breach, *dear friends…*" When was the last time you were three months behind delivery on an important project and your boss called you a dear friend? If there is no inclusion then there is separation. You and Them. You, the boss who knows what they should have done, and Them, the "troops", who have not done it. This saps energy. What the demotivated need is a sense that "we're in this together".

Next, Henry reminds his troops that a push is on:

In peace there's nothing so becomes a man
As modest stillness and humility,
But when the blast of war blows in our ears,
Then imitate the action of the tiger.

He requires a different energy than in peacetime, but he also reminds them that if they succeed they will be one step nearer to peace. Henry lets them know the push is for now, in war, not forever. In fact, the more energy they muster now, the quicker they can get back to a little "stillness and humility".

The habitual Warriors among us forget to think about peace. We keep asking for more energy, more commitment, better results, faster... without any let up or time for rest and relaxation. This is simply not sustainable and can quickly cause burn out. It implies that if the troops meet the target in the short term we will give them a bigger target in the long term. Where's the motivation in that? Don't punish people who work hard and get results.

THE RIGHT IMAGE CHANGES THE ENERGY

The key to re-motivation is effective use of imagery. Henry does not simply tell his troops where to go (they know that already), he tells them how they can be successful when they get there:

... imitate the action of the tiger.
Stiffen the sinews, conjure up the blood,
Disguise fair nature with hard-favoured rage.
Then lend the eye a terrible aspect,
Let it pry through the portage of the head
Like the brass cannon, let the brow o'erwhelm it...
Now set the teeth and stretch the nostril wide,
Hold hard the breath, and bend up every spirit
To his full height. On on...

The language itself serves to wake people up. If you then actually try to put the images into the body, it doubles the effect. This is a very similar idea to the "active imagination" techniques used in psychology. "See" the desired result first, then think what energy you need to achieve it, then imagine yourself doing it, then do it.

> I tried this in our rehearsal room with a bunch of tired actors who hadn't had their first coffee break. I asked them to imagine everything that Henry was telling them to do – and try and actually do it in their bodies: imitate the action of a tiger, stiffen the sinews, summon up the blood, lend the eye a terrible aspect, set the teeth, stretch the nostril wide, hold hard the breath, bend up every spirit to its full height... At the end of the speech I asked them how they felt and they said "Just tell us where to go!"

The image can make it real. It is one of the great human gifts, the ability to see an image and internalize it. The "owning" of an image in this way does something inside, as if by magic. The field of sports psychology knows this well. There is hardly a professional athlete nowadays who does not visualize the desired outcome before starting.

The most feared warrior band of all times, "the Berserkers", took this to the extreme, and prayed that the spirits of wild animals would possess them in battle. The image became so real that many who fought them would report that beasts had set upon them. If you really take the image on board it will change your energy. The right change of energy can change the result.

FINDING THE RIGHT IMAGE

The impassioned and image-led speech is best used sparingly. If Henry had hit the troops with a different version of "Once more unto the breach..." every day for three months it would, of course, have become a cliché, a source of jokes. Timing is crucial. It will take some Warrior courage to stand and deliver in the right way, and it takes the Medicine Woman's imagination to come up with the right image to deliver. ("I want you to act like pussy cats" wouldn't have served Henry so well.)

Management-speak has done its best to kill interesting and imaginative language at work, but a leader who needs to motivate others will need some.

The trick is to find an image that means something to *you*. Borrowing from others – even Shakespeare – doesn't have the same effect.

> Think of your own situation. Then think what it reminds you of – outside work. Find the metaphor or image that best fits the situation. "See" the image in your mind in as much detail as you can. Then think how you would describe it to others. Then check if it stimulates your imagination and motivates you. If it does, the chances are you can use it to motivate others, provided you can summon the energy you feel when you are motivated as you deliver it to others.

It does not matter whether your audience shares an interest in the subject you draw your image from. For example, it doesn't take a keen football fan to understand; "I want us to work together more as a team. Don't get held back from following things through just because it isn't your usual position. If you get the ball, run with it. See if you can finish it yourself. Meanwhile someone else drops back and covers for you. But don't wait to be asked. Work for each other, look around and anticipate. Take the chances when they come and we can win every time."

Alternatively, it doesn't take a horticulture expert to interpret this: "We've got the potential to build a beautiful garden here. But we need more communication. At the moment the people holding the seeds of future projects aren't talking to the marketing department who could tell them where to plant them. And they aren't talking to the budget holders to see if there is enough water anyway! It takes all of us to make the garden flower. No one can do it alone."

If the image means something to you, you can make it mean something to someone else. If it doesn't mean something to you, it can come across as fake, then you will be worse off than before. Remember that you will rarely, if ever, motivate everyone (as we will see in the next scene) but if you let this stop you trying you may not motivate anyone.

BACK UP – WHAT STANDS BEHIND US?

> *On, on, you noblest English...*
> *Dishonour not your mothers; now attest*
> *That those whom you called fathers did beget you.*
> *Be copy now to men of grosser blood,*
> *And teach them how to war. And you, good yeomen,*
> *Whose limbs were made in England, show us here*
> *The mettle of your pasture; let us swear*
> *That you are worth your breeding—which I doubt not,*
> *For there is none of you so mean and base*
> *That hath not noble lustre in your eyes.*

What else can you appeal to, to motivate those who have lost their own motivation? If it is not advisable to use the factual truth of the present (20% dead, 30% sick, etc) focus on the past or the future. At different times Henry will use both; here he focuses on the past, to good effect.

He reminds the troops of their lineage. He gets them to think about their ancestors and appeals to an almost universal human wish to make our parents proud. Malidoma Somé, the African medicine man and scholar, speaks of an image used in the Dagara tribe of Bukina Faso when people are facing great challenge. You are invited to think of the spirits of your parents standing behind you, backing you up, then to imagine the four figures of your grandparents standing behind your parents, then your eight great-grandparents behind the grandparents and so on until you can imagine a great triangle of support behind you. Then imagine that all these ancestors are backing you up, urging you forward, blowing their breath and their wishes for success into you. Henry also suggests "We are not facing this challenge alone, the spirits of our forefathers and mothers are here with us, wishing you well".

He finishes with an assumption that the troops are motivated to move forward, that their spirits have been lifted, and calls their attention to that which they all serve:

I see you stand like greyhounds in the slips,
Straining upon the start. The game's afoot.
Follow your spirit, and upon this charge
Cry, "God for Harry, England and Saint George!"

In this scene, Henry starts with the tangible target – the breach – but ends with a line of service that extends far beyond the breach in question; "Harry, England and Saint George!" The soldiers owe their duty to their boss, the King, but he owes his to England, and the country itself is guided by its patron saint, St George ("You're not just doing this for your parents, or for me, we are doing this for our country, and for the great spirit that guides it.")

This is where those who think work is just about making money will fall down. They have nothing else to back them up and therefore little or no understanding of what really motivates people. All they can do is bribe them with big rewards and threaten them with a big stick. Their version of this speech would be a little shorter: "Once more unto the breach and I'll double your bonus; dishonour not your mothers or I'll fire the lot of you!"

Hmmm.

Act 3 • Scene 2

Motivating the cowards

THE STORY

Pistol, Nym, Bardolph and the Boy have made it to France, and have heard Henry's speech from afar. Bardolph's spirits have been raised, for he starts the scene with his own attempt to motivate the others: "On, on, on! To the breach, to the breach!" The friendly coward, Nym, soon dampens his ardour:

Pray thee corporal, stay. The knocks are too hot,
and for mine own part I have not a case of lives!

To which the others readily agree. Until Captain Llewellyn, a Welsh stickler for discipline, enters and chases them off: "God's blood! Up to the breach, you dogs! Avaunt, you cullions!" The Boy is left alone to ponder his plight:

I have observed these three swashers...
They will steal anything, and call it "purchase"...
in Calais they stole a fire shovel. I knew
by that piece of service the men would carry coals.
I must leave them, and seek some better
service. Their villainy goes against my weak stomach,
and therefore I must cast it up.

YOU CAN'T CHANGE EVERYONE...

For all Henry's speechifying, not everyone will be motivated alike. Some old friends may be among those unwilling to take risks to overcome the first obstacles. The cynical realists may well, like Nym, respond to Henry's rallying call with the undeniable truth: "The breach is too hot!"

Through the eyes of the innocent Boy we glimpse the effect on morale of the unenlightened self-interest displayed by the "swashers". They are so addicted to stealing that, in the absence of anything of real value, they stole a fire shovel, causing their comrades to carry coal by hand, even though they were in mid campaign. This youth – although undoubtedly attracted initially by the "cool" attitude of the tavern folk, with their quick wits and quicker fingers – has seen the limitation of their attitude up close. His conclusion is that their villainy will make him sick; he must "seek some better service".

MOTIVATE SMARTER – NOT HARDER

Henry does not concern himself with these shirkers. He delegates to a captain to chase them up. A leader needs to conserve their energy for motivation, and use it effectively. Motivate *smarter* not harder.

A leader does not have to shoulder all the responsibility for motivating the troops, this too can be effectively delegated. Henry is better off inspiring 10 Llewellyn's than 100 Bardolph's, because Llewellyn will pass the inspiration on, any way he can, whereas Bardolph will retreat at the first objection.

A wise leader will focus on personally inspiring some 10% of the people he or she actually needs to be committed to the project in hand. If a 100 people need to be involved in a particular enterprise, focus on 10 of them. But not just any 10, the 10 who have the most authority with and influence over the other 90. These people are often not those highest up the pecking order, but those popular down the pub or in the canteen, or those who organize social activities, union representatives, etc – the 10% that the others are most likely to listen to.

If we carefully select and successfully motivate these 10, each of them

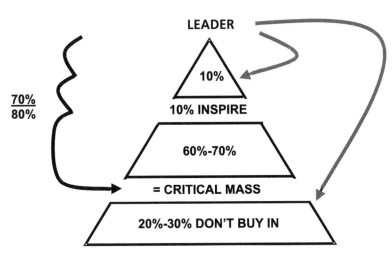

Whom To Motivate

will, on average, motivate six or seven others. When asked about the project in hand these 10 will support it; when others complain; "I hear we've got another bloody go at the breach coming up, that's all we need!" these 10 might respond "Well, I've been talking to the boss and he explained why it's important to keep the pressure up. The sooner we break through the wall the sooner we can get out of the swamp, for which we'd all be grateful."

Our initial 10 plus their six or seven each gives us 70-80% on board. This is a critical mass and the project will move forward, at least to the next step.

Another important point to remember is that in any big project you will never get – nor do you actually ever need – 100% buy in. The cowardly old friends and habitual critics eventually need to be ignored. Some Great Mother characters never get their troops up to the breach because they patiently listen to the Nym's of this world explaining why they don't fancy it, instead of letting Llewellyn and his pike do the necessary. If this sounds like you, practise the following three times a day:

"God's blood! Up to the breaches, you dogs! Avaunt, you cullions!" Eventually even Nym gets this message.

ACT 3 • Scene 3

The four captains

THE STORY

For the first and only time we meet representatives from four nations. Captains from England, Wales, Scotland and Ireland assemble; Gower, Llewellyn, Jamy and MacMorris. All is not going smoothly between the supposed allies.

Llewellyn reports his concerns to Gower: "For look you, the mines is not according to the disciplines of the war – the concavities is not sufficient". He is particularly worried that the Duke of Gloucester "to whom the order of the siege is given" has put his faith in MacMorris: "An Ass (who) has no more directions in the true disciplines of the wars than a puppy dog!"

Captain MacMorris and Captain Jamy enter. Llewellyn wants to discuss the situation but MacMorris is not in a good mood:

> It is no time to discourse, so Chrish save me.
> The town is besieched. And the trumpet call us to the breach,
> and we talk and, be Chrish, do nothing, 'tis shame for us all.

Llewellyn persists and the situation escalates until MacMorris explodes: "So Chrish save me, I will cut off your head!" Gower tries to calm them down: "Gentlemen both, you will mistake each other." But only a trumpet announcing an upcoming parley can interrupt the dispute and the four captains leave, the dispute unresolved:

LLEWELLYN *Captain MacMorris, when there is more better opportunity*
to be required, look you, I will be so bold as to tell you
I know the disciplines of war. And there is an end.

CONFLICTS OF CHARACTER

Captains can be unified under one leader, and yet in conflict amongst themselves. Particularly when things don't go well for an extended period of time, human nature dictates that we look around for someone to blame. There will be times when this scrutiny can keep people on a useful edge and improve their work ("co-opetition" is a current notion related to this, combining co-operation with competition), and there are times when it simply adds to their stress – as it does here to MacMorris.

We are all inclined to talk to others the way we like to be talked to. This works when those others share the same character preference as us, but it can fail when they don't. Llewellyn, operating from the Good King with his memorized book of rules and disciplines, doesn't have a clue how to talk to MacMorris, who is improvizing under terrible conditions and searching for any way through (and therefore operating from Warrior and Medicine Woman). Although Llewellyn probably has some good ideas, and a genuine wish to solve the problem, he is unable to communicate effectively. His attempt at naysaying is received by MacMorris first as unhelpful criticism, and secondly as personal insult. The result is a fight that distracts all four captains from the task at hand.

Only when we feel comfortable playing all four characters do we have a full repertoire. Then we can switch roles to suit the person and situation in front of us. Henry does this throughout the play; Llewellyn learns it only at the end (see Act 5 Scene 1).

DELEGATION AS PROTECTION

We get to see this conflict, but Henry doesn't. Just as it was Llewellyn who dealt with the cowards, it is the Duke of Gloucester who must deal with the captains.

Later, it will be important for Henry to disguise himself and hear what the troops are thinking as he deliberates in his "dark night". It is probably equally important that he *does not* hear all the arguments between the captains. As the following example illustrates, a leader needs to decide which burdens to carry, and which to protect themselves from.

> A deputy chief executive of a local council was tasked with seeing through a huge restructuring process that was having a significant impact on layers of middle management. These folk were changing roles, some were losing jobs, and in the middle of the transition it got pretty sticky – erstwhile friends competing for new positions, a lot of political manoeuvring and some emotional blackmail. The deputy went to her boss and said that she was handling the situation and it would eventually calm down, but in the meantime did he want to know the details of how things were going. He said no; "I can't do what I need to do and carry the emotional burden of others at the same time."

There is a difference between ignoring the impact of decisions on others, and not taking the brunt of the burden once the decision has been made.

Some leaders get all macho with a "no pain no gain" attitude, some get weighed down with the concerns of others. The latter may make it too difficult to keep on doing what has to be done. At this point the project was underway and the boss needed to keep his focus on what was coming. The deputy was the right person to deal with the emotional and political realities of those involved further down the line.

SEEING BENEATH THE SURFACE

The four captains also have a symbolic significance. Historically this meeting could not have occurred; the only Scots at the battle of Agincourt were 200 mercenaries fighting for the French! So Shakespeare is again distorting the actual to create a mythic truth.

There is an ancient myth of the Grail Kingdom that includes England, Ireland, Scotland, Wales and France. According to legend every so often a hero will arise whose destiny is to reunite these five great nations and create a new golden age. Shakespeare draws on mythology throughout his works so it is unlikely to be accidental that here he shows representatives of four nations attempting to win the fifth. It is a hint that the play is constructed to be seen from different levels. Some in the audience will see it as entertainment, some as history and – those who can read the symbols – will see it as allegory. One such allegorical tale is of the prodigal son (Henry) who rises from nothing (the tavern) to unite former enemies (nobles and captains) in a common goal (reclaiming France) to start a time of great prosperity (the golden age of the Grail Kingdom).

An allegory serves to invite those who engage with it to consider the symbolic and internal significance of apparently external events. So the four captains represent four quarters of a whole (much like the four characters or the four elements); the hero's task is to unite them while keeping their diversity alive. There will be other times in the play when the symbolic significance on stage is as important as the human interaction. These clues are carefully hidden, and will not be seen unless they are looked for.

I once met the philosopher and writer Sir Laurens Van der Post. We talked about what it takes to be a "man of history"; he said the sign of a great person – someone able to change the course of history for a community or a nation – was the ability to sense the mythic flow of time. To see the surface of history running one way and sense the undercurrent flowing in a different direction. Then to harness the undercurrent until it changes the surface.

There are only a few in each age who master this on a grand scale – Mahatma Ghandi, Nelson Mandela and Mikhail Gorbachov in recent history – but anyone in a leadership role can at least hold the possibility that what they see on the surface is not the whole story. We can all try and imagine ourselves looking back at the present from a time in the future and seeing what was really going on "then". Historians do this with the benefit of hindsight; those who change history do it now.

ACT 3 • Scene 4

Changing tactics, changing strategy

THE STORY

The Governor of the besieged Harfleur has called a parley. Henry arrives outside the gates of the town and begins the talking:

> This is the latest parle we will admit...
> As I am a soldier,
> A name that in my thoughts becomes me best,
> If I begin the batt'ry once again
> I will not leave the half-achievèd Harfleur
> Till in her ashes she lie burièd.
> The gates of mercy shall be all shut up...

What is it then to me if impious war
Arrayed in flames like to the prince of fiends
Do with his smirched complexion all fell feats
Enlinked to waste and desolation?
What is 't to me, when you yourselves are cause,
If your pure maidens fall into the hand
Of hot and forcing violation?
What rein can hold licentious wickedness
When down the hill he holds his fierce career?
We may as bootless spend our vain command
Upon th' enragèd soldiers in their spoil
As send precepts to the leviathan
To come ashore. Therefore, you men of Harfleur,
Take pity of your town and of your people
Whiles yet my soldiers are in my command...
If not—why, in a moment look to see
The blind and bloody soldier with foul hand
Defile the locks of your shrill-shrieking daughters;
Your fathers taken by the silver beards,
And their most reverend heads dashed to the walls;
Your naked infants spitted upon pikes,
Whiles the mad mothers with their howls confused
Do break the clouds, as did the wives of Jewry
At Herod's bloody-hunting slaughtermen.
What say you? Will you yield, and this avoid?
Or, guilty in defence, be thus destroyed.

The Governor appears on the wall of the town to yield the town. The King asks him to open the gates, then turns to Exeter, his senior noble:

Fortify (Harfleur) strongly 'gainst the French.
Use mercy to them all. For us, dear uncle,
The winter coming on, and sickness growing
Upon our soldiers, we will retire to Calais.

CHANGING TACTICS – PAINTING NEGATIVE PICTURES

For three months Henry has fought against Harfleur with weapons, now he seeks to persuade with words. His previous speech motivated the troops into the breach and their renewed vigour seems to have paid off; the Governor calls a temporary truce, and Henry senses the possibility of victory. He does not, however, wait for the Governor to put possible terms and conditions on the table, but speaks his mind first and forcefully.

The images he draws in this speech are terrible. Some people choose to see it as proof that Henry is a tyrant. I believe he demonstrates another quality of an inspirational leader; the ability to paint such an effective negative view of the future that he stops that potential future from occurring. This is a key influencing skill.

> Think about your own experience. Have you ever been involved in a project that you sensed early on was not going to work, and others sensed the same thing? Yet no one knew how to stop it, so it carried on, until its foreseen failure, at which point people said; "I knew that was going to happen, I could have told you it wasn't going to work." But they didn't, at least not before it was too late.

Henry demonstrates how to do it. He senses one potential future for the Governor's town and describes it in detail, without pulling any punches in the images he uses:

> *Impious war... Arrayed in flames... the prince of fiends*
> *waste and desolation... hot and forcing violation...*
> *licentious wickedness... fierce career... enragèd soldiers*
> *The blind and bloody soldier... foul hand*
> *Defile... shrill-shrieking daughters;*
> *Your fathers... heads dashed to the walls;*
> *Your naked infants spitted upon pikes...*
> *mad mothers... howls confused...*
> *Herod's bloody-hunting slaughtermen...*

Powerful stuff. Sometimes in seminars I ask participants to imagine that they are the decision-makers being addressed by Henry. In role as the

"Men of Harfleur" it is hard not to be persuaded that surrender is the only option.

By using these brutal words to paint horrible pictures in the Governor's mind, Henry actually prevents the negative potential. In other words, he uses violent words to stop violent deeds. The Governor "sees" the future that Henry describes and takes action to stop it becoming reality. He surrenders while Henry's soldiers are still in his control.

It takes courage to stick our neck out and say something is going to fail. But if we truly think it is, then we need to become effective Naysayers – and paint a negative picture of the future clearly enough that others will recognize it and change their minds, before it is too late.

UNDERSTANDING THE DARK SIDE OF HUMAN NATURE

People often ask: "If the Governor did not surrender would Henry actually carry out the threat?" Of course, we will never know, but I would say it was not *his* threat, it was his reading of the future, of what might happen, the potential threat posed by angry and frustrated soldiers. The possibility of Henry's army actually losing control, and of him being unable to restrain them, is as negative a future for him as the Commander-in-Chief as the destruction of the town would be for the Governor. Both leaders would lose control of what they were leading/serving. To stop both happening could be seen as a win-win.

There is, unfortunately, a truth in the picture he paints. It is part of the dark side of human nature to punish those who physically resist us – particularly when we have decided that a particular course of action is the right one. Henry is more likely to have learnt this in the tavern than in a castle. Working with some police commanders recently reinforced his point. They would caution officers against using excessive force, but the more robust the resistance to arrest, the more robust the arrest became. If officers knew a particular subject was responsible for injuring their friends, no leader could stop their troops from twisting the offending arm harder than necessary. The sporting equivalent occurs in retaliatory tackles on football and rugby pitches every weekend.

Therefore the longer Henry's troops spend outside the gates of Harfleur watching their mates get injured or killed, the more retribution they are likely to seek. Henry foresees that frustration reaching a level at which he would be unable to control it – when the impulse to "payback" overcomes training and discipline.

The corporate version of this can be seen in resisted aggressive takeovers. The more the targeted prey resists, the quicker it is broken up and sold off after eventual surrender. Senior managers surplus to requirements tell stories of coming back from lunch to find access codes changed, their belongings thrown in a box and family pictures cracked from the excessive zeal of the packers.

A leader who recognizes the less honourable impulses in human beings is more likely to prevent such unfair punishment.

CHANGING CHARACTER, CHANGING STRATEGY

At different times in this short scene Henry plays each of our four leadership characters. The Medicine Woman imagines the potential future. The Warrior speaks strongly to penetrate the defences of those who have resisted a three-month siege. (Henry acknowledges it as his favourite character: "As I am a soldier, a name that in my thoughts becomes me best".) The Great Mother requires good treatment for all the inhabitants of the town: "Use mercy to them all." And finally, having avoided the negative future, the Good King rethinks his strategy:

> For us, dear uncle,
> The winter coming on, and sickness growing
> Upon our soldiers, we will retire to Calais.
> Tonight in Harfleur will we be your guest;
> Tomorrow for the march are we addressed.

In this brief summary we learn of Henry's first change of plan in the play. Up till now he has pursued his intentions in a straight line; plan, act and persevere. Here we see the sensible realist who knows when the original

Strategy As A Process

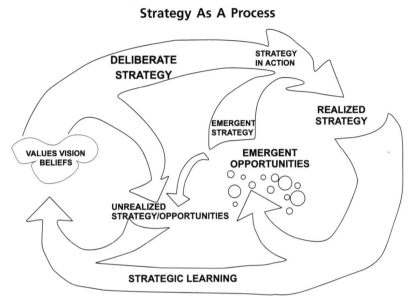

(Developed by Mintzberg and Moncrief)

intention is no longer workable. Let us look at a modern model of strategy as a process (see above).

Henry has set his strategy in line with his vision, values and beliefs. He pursues his deliberate strategy and lands at Harfleur. His primary objective, to take the town in a week, soon becomes unrealized; he follows his strategy in action for three more months and now, finally, takes Harfleur – a realized first strategic aim. However, the deliberate strategy he set out with (Paris by Christmas) is not viable.

A lesser leader might make one of two apparently obvious choices. An addicted Warrior would find it hard to admit any kind of defeat; he might push on to Paris, regardless of winter weather and sick soldiers. A compulsive Great Mother might retreat to England so the sick can be properly looked after. However, this would create a perception of failure that might come back to haunt her. (Remember Jimmy Carter's failed attempt to rescue hostages – somehow the fact that the helicopters' engines clogged with sand became seen as weak leadership.)

Henry finds a third way. A strategic withdrawal to the port town of Calais – one of the few remaining English territories in France. The troops can rest up over winter, he can access more resources from England, and the offensive can restart in the spring. Neither forward attack nor backward retreat – but a sideways move.

This is an emergent opportunity, unplanned but spontaneously available, and it becomes his emergent strategy. There are times to treat barriers as obstacles to be overcome, and times to treat them as signs to find another way. Reading the barriers correctly is part luck, part judgement – that ability to look beneath the surface, and to know when your people need a break.

ACT 3 • Scene 5

Meeting the princess

THE STORY

We meet Princess Katherine of France, attended by her lady-in-waiting, Alice. Katherine asks Alice for an English lesson saying: "Il faut que j'apprenne parler". The first lesson begins; Katherine is particularly keen to learn how to name the different parts of the body...

COMMENT

Katherine does not seem to be as concerned as the rest of her family about the current invasion. Nor does she seem in any particular doubt about the outcome. She is learning English – the better, presumably, to converse with Henry, at some undisclosed time in the future.

Nor is it an accident that we meet her at this point in the play. Henry has just achieved his first victory; the first walls have been breeched...

and out walks a princess. Symbolically, a princess in myth can be seen to represent what Carl Jung named the Anima, described by Tom Chetwynd in *A Dictionary of Symbols* as follows: "This figure is a personification of the heart rather than the head: the feelings, and especially the feeling of being alive, which gets lost sometimes. It is the source of receptiveness and sensitivity."

Katherine is the living embodiment of the Dynamic Feminine Medicine Woman energy in the play. She is a refreshing presence, sensitive to future possibilities and receptive to new learning. She will lead Henry towards a transformation in Act 5.

Another mythic reference is emerging; St George, the Dragon and the imprisoned Maiden. Henry has already called upon "Saint George" in Act 3 Scene 1, and now we meet the Maiden (Princess Katherine). The Dragon will come, in the form of 40,000 fresh French soldiers, even at this point in the story gathering at the French Court. The French, as Canterbury told us in Act 1 Scene 2, are denying anyone the right to inherit through the feminine line. Henry, as the hero, in the line of service that ends with St George, must overcome the Dragon that guards the cave where the Princess waits.

We do not meet the Princess for long, and as she cannot talk in our tongue, she must remain something of a mystery for now. But at least we know she is there, in the "cave", and she wants to learn how to communicate with us.

ACT 3 Scene 6

The French response

THE STORY

The French Court is ashamed of the loss of Harfleur; they have gathered a huge army and plan their response:

KING CHARLES *Bar Harry England... rush on his host...*
You have power enough,
And in a captive chariot into Rouen
Bring him our prisoner...

CONSTABLE *I am sure when he shall see our army*
He'll offer us his ransom.

KING CHARLES *Therefore, Lord Constable, haste on Montjoy,*
And let him say to England that we send
To know what willing ransom he will give...
And quickly bring us word of England's fall.

COMMENT

The French are acting in response to Henry; the blow to their pride causes a knee jerk reaction. They do not think through a strategy but rely on the sheer weight of numbers to win the day. The Constable and King Charles both assume Henry will give up, the only thing to be decided is how much ransom they will seek as reparation for Harfleur. "Know your enemy" goes the saying; the French don't bother.

ACT 3 • Scene 7

Facing the challenge

THE STORY

The Welsh and English captains, Llewellyn and Gower, meet to share information. Their troops are holding a bridgehead that could enable the English to get ahead of the pursuing French forces. They are interrupted by Pistol who asks for Llewellyn's help. Bardolph has been caught stealing a cross from a church, a hangable offence in Henry's army, and the Duke of Exeter has ordered his immediate death. Llewellyn replies; "if he were my brother I would desire the Duke to put him to execution". Pistol goes off cursing. Henry enters and requests an update:

	What men have you lost, Llewellyn?
LLEWELLYN	*I think the Duke hath lost never a man,*
	but one that is like to be executed for robbing
	a church, one Bardolph, if your majesty know the man...
HENRY	*We would have all such offenders so cut off,*
	and we here give express charge that in our marches
	through the country there be nothing compelled from
	the villages, nothing taken but paid for, none of the
	French upbraided or abused in disdainful language. For
	when lenity and cruelty play for a kingdom, the gentler
	gamester is the soonest winner.

The French Herald, Montjoy, enters with an ultimatum from the French king:

> *England shall repent. Bid*
> *him therefore consider of his ransom, which must*
> *proportion the losses we have borne, the subjects we*
> *have lost, the disgrace we have digested... To*
> *this add defiance, and tell him for conclusion he hath*
> *betrayed his followers, whose condemnation is*
> *pronounced.*

The offer is simple: give up now and be fined (but survive), or fight tomorrow (and die). Henry responds:

> *Tell thy King I do not seek him now,*
> *But could be willing to march on to Calais*
> *Without impeachment, for to say the sooth—*
> *Though 'tis no wisdom to confess so much*

119

Unto an enemy of craft and vantage—
My people are with sickness much enfeebled,
My numbers lessened, and those few I have
Almost no better than so many French;
Who when they were in health—I tell thee herald,
I thought upon one pair of English legs
Did march three Frenchmen. Yet forgive me, God,
That I do brag thus. This your air of France
Hath blown that vice in me. I must repent.
Go, therefore, tell thy master here I am;
My ransom is this frail and worthless trunk,
My army but a weak and sickly guard.
Yet, God before, tell him we will come on,
Though France himself and such another neighbour
Stand in our way... And so, Montjoy, fare you well.
The sum of all our answer is but this:
We would not seek a battle as we are,
Nor as we are we say we will not shun it.
So tell your master.

Montjoy leaves and Gloucester confides to Henry that he hopes the French do not attack now. Henry replies:

We are in God's hand, brother, not in theirs.
March to the bridge. It now draws toward night.
Beyond the river we'll encamp ourselves,
And on tomorrow. Bid them march away.

THE CHALLENGE WITHIN

Here Henry meets a big test. Does he allow an old friend, Bardolph, to be executed or does he intervene and bend the rules for old time's sake? Exeter has ordered the execution, not knowing of the relationship of the criminal to the King. If Henry were to contradict his General he would undermine Exeter's authority with his troops. And the rule not to steal from the French is part of Henry's larger plan. He wishes to rule his new territory in peace and knows that "when lenity and cruelty play for a kingdom, the gentler gamester is the soonest winner." If he lets Bardolph off, other troops may take licence to steal and create resentment among the people he seeks to lead. He doesn't really have a choice. Or rather he made the choice when he left the tavern for the last time, accepted the crown and banished his old friends from his company. It is a hard but necessary sacrifice, for the sake of the greater good.

MANAGERS SOLVE PROBLEMS – LEADERS MANAGE DILEMMAS

The Robert K Greenleaf Center for Servant Leadership in America identified four "Right versus Right dilemmas". These are the leadership issues for which there is no simple answer; one could find different reasons to answer either yes or no. The leader has to make a choice – rather than a simple decision.

Short term vs long term: You cannot prioritize the short term and the long term simultaneously. Yet a leader of a public company will feel the pressure to maximize short-term returns for investors and sustain long-term growth. At any given moment he or she will have to prioritize one over the other. And at each of these moments there would be arguments opposing the chosen priority. Yet the choice must be made and the leader held accountable.

Individual vs community: Do we decide to enhance the life or prospects of one extremely talented individual, or do we share the available resources among a group? (This dilemma is keenly felt in Britain's National Health Service where senior managers may have to balance one £100,000 life-saving operation against 10 £10,000 limb-saving operations.) There is no simple "right", but a choice has to be made.

Truth vs loyalty: When do we treat mistakes as learning opportunities and when do we reveal that a rule has been broken? If we have invested a lot of time and money in training someone should we disclose mistakes that a boss might judge as inexcusable? Do we keep quiet to remain loyal to a team member or tell the truth and blow the whistle? Each situation will have to be weighed by those in a leadership role.

Justice vs mercy: When do you forgive and when do you punish to the letter of the law? Henry forgives the drunk who rails at him in Southampton, but sentences the traitors to death, and chooses not to interfere with Bardolph's execution. In Act 4 we will see him forgiving a soldier who says the King is a liar. In each case either side could be justified using different arguments. As a leader Henry makes his choices and sticks to them.

All four of these dilemmas are reflected in the "Bardolph decision". On this occasion Henry chooses long term, community, truth and justice. In the short term it would be "easier" to let a man off in the middle of a withdrawing army than to punish him. But in the long term it would send a message to other troops that they could also risk breaking the law. For the individual concerned it would certainly be desirable to bend the rules, but for the overall community it would be dangerous to be seen to be lenient. The truth that Bardolph has broken a clear law with a known and fixed punishment outweighs loyalty to an old friend. In Henry's eyes at this moment the need to be just outweighs the wish to be merciful.

LEARNING TO MAKE THE HARD DECISIONS

Some people say that Henry is cold hearted and therefore not really affected by this decision. Historically this may be true, we will never know, but my experience with the play leads me to disagree.

> You may remember from the discussions around political intelligence in Act 1 that we took the cast of *Henry V* to an old airfield to improvise our way through the story. This included important events that happen before the

play starts and all relevant events that occur off stage during the play itself. (I have found this kind of exercise to be of particular use in preparing a company for the Globe stage, as they have no lighting and no scenery to tell the audience where they are. The actors have to imagine their situation and attempt to transmit this imaginative truth to the audience.)

Mark Rylance, as Henry, had a particular request to play the deathbed scene with his father (from *Henry IV Part 2*), and also to spend time in the tavern with Pistol, Bardolph *et al*, before banishing them for the sake of his promised reformation.

As Mark threw himself wholeheartedly into these two improvizations I could see how difficult it was for Henry. In the tavern he could be more anonymous, one of the lads, having fun and living in the moment. At Court he had to be a prince, ever aware of others and the impression he made on them. In either place it was as if he were denying another part of himself, and when it came to banishing his old friends there was more than a hint of remorse that this was how it had to be.

By the time we came to this scene in Act 3 Henry had grown into the role of King and was making decisions fluidly and effectively. He was supported throughout by his two brothers, Gloucester and Bedford, who, by this stage of rehearsal, had developed into a kind of "carrot and stick" double act; Gloucester emphasizing and supporting the softer, human side of Henry and his leadership, Bedford holding the harder edge. Mark, in role as Henry, found it valuable to have these two sides of leadership externalized and ever present among his close advisors.

When he heard from Llewellyn about Bardolph's imminent death he was visibly taken aback. He looked around to his brothers for advice. Gloucester (the humanitarian) dropped his head, Bedford (the disciplinarian) walked very deliberately up to Henry, holding eye contact all the way, silently reminding the King of his duty to uphold the law. Henry looked down, swallowed hard, looked up, nodded to Bedford and said: "We would have all such offenders so cut off", thus settling the fate of his friend. His whole reply reads:

> *We would have all such offenders so cut off,*
> *and we here give express charge that in our marches*

through the country there be nothing compelled from the villages, nothing taken but paid for, none of the French upbraided or abused in disdainful language. For when lenity and cruelty play for a kingdom, the gentler gamester is the soonest winner.

What made the task of delivering these thoughts even harder was that Bardolph was being marched by, held between two soldiers. As he heard his sentence he wrestled free and threw himself on the ground at Henry's feet pleading for mercy with tears in his eyes. Bedford stepped in and pulled him away while Henry (Mark) had to hold his resolve, not engage with Bardolph and keep talking to the waiting captains. A short time later Bardolph was strung up on a scaffold and Henry commanded all his troops to walk past the swinging gibbet. Henry watched the walk past before finding a brief time alone to kneel and offer a prayer for Bardolph's soul.

Sometimes a leader has to play the tough commanding officer, even when everything inside them is yearning to do the opposite. The hardest decisions of all are those that cause pain to a few whom you know for the sake of many whom you don't know. I found the following real-life example in an old book of First World War poems. The writer expresses his real feelings after composing the necessary letter to the father of a dead soldier.

IN MEMORIAM

For Private D Sutherland killed in action in the German trench, 16 May 1916, and the others who died.

You were only David's father
But I had fifty sons
When we went up in the evening
Under the arch of the guns,
And we came back at twilight –
O God I heard them call
To me for help and pity
That could not help at all.

Oh, never will I forget you,
My men that trusted me,
More my sons than your fathers',
For they could only see
The little helpless babies
And the young men in their pride.
They could not see you dying,
And hold you while you died.

Happy and young and gallant,
They saw their first born go,
But not the strong limbs broken
And the beautiful men brought low,
The piteous writhing bodies,
They screamed "Don't leave me, sir"
For they were only your fathers
But I was your officer.

(By EA Mackintosh [killed in action, 1916])

While nothing in modern organizational life will match the horrendous responsibility felt by EA Mackintosh, most leaders will, at times, have to make decisions that impact negatively on others.

> Sarah, a senior manager in a TV production company, knew that Peter, a key member of her staff, was under-performing and incapable of the necessary improvement. She knew all the arguments that should make their next meeting the beginning of the end of his current job, but somehow she kept stopping herself from doing anything. The thought of facing him and saying "You're not up to it, I'm sorry" was too difficult. Other senior managers were clearly getting frustrated with the lack of direct action. The implication was clear. If the situation continued, and other staff had to pick up the slack for another's incompetence, morale would deteriorate, as would trust in their leader. Sarah needed to recognize that the good of the many outweighed the wish of the one. The necessary action would be in the long-term interest of all, including the worker out of depth in his current position. Sarah became aware of her resistance to doing

anything that might cause others to dislike her. We role played her metaphorically putting on some "armour" and summoning up some Warrior energy to brave the first meeting. After this, Sarah realized what she had been avoiding and why. It was a lesson in the occasional need to wear a leader's face, rather than a personal face – and was a similar struggle to the one I witnessed Henry going through and winning at the abandoned airfield.

THE CHALLENGE FROM WITHOUT

There's no rest for the wicked – or for the good leader approaching crisis. No sooner has Henry passed the "Bardolph test" than he has to face a more threatening challenge. Montjoy arrives with an ultimatum from the French King to give up now and pay a huge ransom (but live), or fight tomorrow (but die). Henry receives the ultimatum in full view of his troops. He has no choice but to respond in public, which he does brilliantly, managing both to rebuff the challenge and build up morale simultaneously. First he delivers a clear instruction that gives him the semblance of control:

> *Turn thee back*
> *And tell thy King I do not seek him now,*
> *But could be willing to march on to Calais*
> *Without impeachment.*

As if he had a choice in the matter! Then he makes an odd confession:

> *Though 'tis no wisdom to confess so much*
> *Unto an enemy of craft and vantage—*
> *My people are with sickness much enfeebled,*
> *(And) my numbers lessened...*

He admits weakness only to turn it around:

> *... and those few I have*
> *Almost no better than so many French;*
> *Who when they were in health—I tell thee herald,*
> *I thought upon one pair of English legs*
> *Did march three Frenchmen.*

He does not even need numbers to beat his enemy. The listening troops hear Henry's confidence and his high estimation of their value. Now he seems to backtrack:

> *Yet forgive me, God,*
> *That I do brag thus.*

Then he explains the reason to score another point over the pompous messenger:

> *This your air of France*
> *Hath blown that vice in me. I must repent.*

He publicly refuses to ransom himself out of danger:

> *Go, therefore, tell thy master here I am;*
> *My ransom is this frail and worthless trunk,*
> *My army but a weak and sickly guard.*

And adds a simple and determined commitment:

> *Yet, God before, tell him we will come on,*
> *Though France himself and such another neighbour*
> *Stand in our way.*

Henry's firm belief that he is in a line of service and doing the right thing will overcome any obstacle, even if two armies opposed him, even with his "sickly guard":

The sum of all our answer is but this:
We would not seek a battle as we are,
Nor as we are we say we will not shun it.
So tell your master.

He puts the ball squarely back in the French court, but with no concessions given. After Montjoy has left, we hear Gloucester's concern; "I hope they will not come upon us now." Henry assures him that the situation is not in the control of the French; he reinforces the sense of a greater purpose at work: "We are in God's hand, brother, not in theirs." He ends with the kind of clear decision making that people (even "nobles") need to see in a crisis:

March to the bridge. It now draws toward night.
Beyond the river we'll encamp ourselves,
And on tomorrow. Bid them march away.

Henry has faced the challenges so far. Now he will enter a "long dark night" before he actually decides whether to fight or not. He cannot show any doubt or hesitation to the troops, but he will need to face his own inner fears and doubts before he can help his troops overcome theirs.

When we reach this stage of a big project it feels as if everything is conspiring against us, and that there is no successful way through and out. It is time to clarify if we really think we are doing the right thing, if we really are the right person to be doing it and, most importantly, if we really have the right to ask others to make sacrifices for our mission.

ACT 3 • Scene 8

The enemy awaits

THE STORY

In the French camp the Lord Constable, Lord Rambures, the Duke of Orleans and the Dauphin wait impatiently for the morning to come and battle to begin. They compare armour and horses; each boasting theirs is the best. The Dauphin is about to recite a sonnet he wrote for his horse, when Orleans teases him that he is treating his horse like his mistress. The Dauphin gets upset and leaves. The others continue talking:

ORLEANS   *The Dauphin longs for morning.*

RAMBURES   *He longs to eat the English.*

ORLEANS   *He never did harm that I heard of.*

CONSTABLE *Nor will do none tomorrow.*

ORLEANS   *I know him to be valiant.*

CONSTABLE *I was told that by one that knows him better than you.*

ORLEANS   *What's he?*

CONSTABLE *Marry, he told me so himself, and he said he cared not who knew it!*

A Messenger tells them the English lie within 1,500 paces of their tents:

CONSTABLE *If the English had any apprehension, they would run away.*

ORLEANS   *That they lack—for if their heads had any intellectual armour, they could never wear such heavy headpieces... It is now two o'clock. But let me see—by ten we shall have each a hundred Englishmen.*

COMMENT

While Henry prepares for an inward journey at the beginning of Act 4, the French concentrate on externals. They seem more concerned with who has the "flashiest car" than the impending battle. They are happy to mock each other and the enemy. At this point they appear incapable of taking anything seriously.

Act 4

The "dark night of the soul"

Henry V (Mark Rylance).

Photo: John Tramper

Act 4 shows Henry going through the long dark night before the battle. He makes time and space to manage his own fears and feel the burden of leadership before being able to inspire his troops to an apparently miraculous victory, against the odds.

> *I and my bosom must debate awhile,*
> *And then I would no other company...*
> *Upon the King.*
> *"Let us our lives, our souls, our debts, our care-full wives,*
> *Our children, and our sins, lay on the King."*
> *We must bear all. O hard condition,*
> *Twin-born with greatness: subject to the breath*
> *Of every fool, whose sense no more can feel*
> *But his own wringing. What infinite heartsease*
> *Must kings neglect that private men enjoy?"*

ACT 4 • Chorus

Visible leadership

THE STORY

CHORUS *Now entertain conjecture of a time*
When creeping murmur and the poring dark
Fills the wide vessel of the universe.
From camp to camp through the foul womb of night
The hum of either army stilly sounds,
That the fixed sentinels almost receive
The secret whispers of each other's watch.
Fire answers fire... and from the tents
The armourers, accomplishing the knights,
With busy hammers closing rivets up,
Give dreadful note of preparation.
The country cocks do crow, the clocks do toll
And the third hour of drowsy morning name.
Proud of their numbers and secure in soul,
The confident and overlusty French
Do the low-rated English play at dice,
And chide the cripple tardy-gaited night,
Who like a foul and ugly witch doth limp
So tediously away. The poor condemnèd English,
Like sacrifices, by their watchful fires
Sit patiently and inly ruminate
The morning's danger; and their gesture sad,
Investing lank lean cheeks and war-worn coats,
Presented them unto the gazing moon
So many horrid ghosts. O now, who will behold
The royal captain of this ruined band...
For forth he goes and visits all his host,
Bids them good morrow with a modest smile

133

And calls them brothers, friends, and countrymen.
Upon his royal face there is no note
How dread an army hath enrounded him...
                    He freshly looks
With cheerful semblance and sweet majesty,
That every wretch, pining and pale before,
Beholding him, plucks comfort from his looks.
A largess universal, like the sun,
His liberal eye doth give to everyone,
Thawing cold fear, that mean and gentle all
Behold, as may unworthiness define,
A little touch of Harry in the night.

THE "ROYAL FACE"

This is, to me, one of the most evocative descriptions in all of Shakespeare. The fires, the secret whispers, the busy hammers armouring the knights, the confident and impatient French, the war-worn English, like sacrifices, waiting to die, and their Royal Captain who walks in their midst "thawing cold fear..."

There is plenty to be afraid of, and this is where Henry shows he is capable of "MBWA" – Management By Walking About. In the midst of a crisis, the logical place to be is in Headquarters where one has the greatest access to information, and from where decisions can be most quickly communicated. *But* it is not the right place to be (at least not all the time). The walking about is hard because we are used to being able to fix things and here we cannot fix anything. We have to hold something intangible for others. We may just need to be seen – and to be seen not to panic:

Upon his royal face there is no note
How dread an army hath enrounded him.

Shakespeare intuitively emphasizes that Henry is showing his *"royal* face", as if to tell us it is not his personal face. Back in Act 1 we found that part of the role of royalty was to be seen – hence the yearly "ambit" of their territory. This role is especially important when it seems as if our project cannot succeed, when it feels that we must admit defeat, or find another way, or find another job, or whatever. This role of Visible Leadership – showing the royal face in a crisis – is one of the most difficult roles to inhabit. It is exactly the point at which acting skills need to be carefully balanced with real feeling. Sometimes an effective leader needs to be an effective actor.

THE GOOD LEADER AS GOOD ACTOR

When Henry puts on his "royal face" and "freshly looks with cheerful semblance and sweet majesty" he is acting, but necessarily so because, as we shall see, this acting will make the desired result more probable.

Henry's performance starts with simply being there. Three o'clock in the morning the night before the biggest decision, the biggest battle of your entire life, would you want to be walking round meeting the troops? I don't think so. If you are anything like me you'd rather be tucked up in bed with a blanket over your head, crying "Help!" But if you don't show up in a crisis the troops think the worst: "They're just looking after themselves", "We mean nothing to them", "They're planning their own escape route", etc.

Just showing up won't do it either. Remember what you will be meeting:

> *The poor condemnèd English,*
> *Like sacrifices, by their watchful fires*
> *Sit patiently and inly ruminate*
> *The morning's danger; (and) their gesture sad,*
> *Investing lank lean cheeks and war-worn coats...*
> *(Like) so many horrid ghosts.*

How on earth can you make a difference to them? You could try and give them a positive spin. But if Henry were to stride about saying "Only

40,000 French out there tomorrow chaps. Should be a good day!" no one would believe him. Worse, they may stop trusting him. On the other hand, if he were to say what he really feels, as he does when he is alone with his brother (in Act 4 Scene 1); "'tis true that we are in great danger", that wouldn't help the troops either. That's more information than they need. So he must, once again, find a third way, somewhere in-between the private truth and the public lie. The great Brazilian theatre practitioner Augusto Boal speaks clearly about the purpose of acting in his book *Playing Boal – Theatre, Therapy, Activism*: "Theatre is the first discovery of humankind. Theatre emerges in the moment in which the human being recognizes that he can see himself (mirror), recognizes who he is and is not, and imagines who he could become."

It is this imagination of a future possibility that a good leader can then inhabit and hold as a mirror for others. The imagination can make it real.

I learnt this for myself in an acting class at UCLA. I was working with another actor on a scene and our Director asked him to come into the room angry and slam the door. The actor said; "I can't slam the door because I am not feeling angry." To which the Director replied: "If you slam the door, you will feel angry." In other words, pretending to be angry enough to slam the door and then physically inhabiting the energy required to slam the door will put an angry energy into your body. What starts as pretence ends up with the desired outcome.

A similar process occurs for Henry. He pretends to be confident enough to go out and meet the troops:

> He... visits all his host,
> Bids them good morrow with a modest smile
> And calls them brothers, friends, and countrymen.
> Upon his royal face there is no note
> How dread an army hath enrounded him...
> He freshly looks
> With cheerful semblance and sweet majesty.

136

But the "semblance", the seeming cheerfulness, becomes reality. The apparent confidence is infectious and has the desired effect:

> *...every wretch, pining and pale before,*
> *Beholding him, plucks comfort from his looks.*

By acting confidently Henry actually makes his troops feel more confident. The acting can make it real. This is one of the real values of the mythodramatic approach in action. If we stay with the known and the logical, "I don't feel confident so I can't look confident in front of my troops", the troops will remain unconfident. Our "truth" becomes a self-fulfilling prophecy. It is the "as if" imaginative approach that can change a hopeless future into the magic of "A little touch of Harry in the night..."

PLAYING IT RIGHT

Henry finds the third way, neither lying, nor revealing the whole truth. He walks the tightrope between the tough-it-out Warrior and the caring, sharing Great Mother with consummate skill. And it isn't easy.

> In the longer Mythodrama seminars we often invite leaders to get into role for this part of the story; find a relevant equivalent in their own leadership practice, cast others as their "troops" and then try it out, rehearse the visible leadership.
>
> A group of troops meet and get into character — fearful workers unsure of their future. Then the leader walks into the scene and interacts with them. Many of the leaders feel themselves shutting down when they see the concern in the eyes of their troops. They either want to leave immediately or stay and make it better. But if they are drawn into conversation they regret it. They have no solutions to offer so the longer the talking goes on the more of a hole they dig for themselves, and the more worried the troops become.

Henry, on the other hand, again holds the appropriate middle ground. He is able to give of himself:

137

A largess universal, like the sun,
His liberal eye doth give to everyone,
Thawing cold fear.

This generosity is part of the Great Mother character, who will put herself out to ensure the greater comfort of others. But Henry does not overplay her and get drawn into the uncomfortable conversations:

(He) bids them good morrow with a modest smile
And calls them brothers, friends, and countrymen.

Not lying but not telling the whole truth. Sometimes you can even be honest about what you can't tell them.

> The HR Director of an oil company was privy to some strategic planning scenarios, which would involve redundancies and relocations for many people. Naturally, wherever he went people wanted to know what was happening but he was not at liberty to reveal it. He found the best solution was to be truthful about the extent to which he could be honest. Rather than lying and saying "I don't know", he would say "OK, I do know what is being planned and at the moment there are good reasons why I can't tell you all about it. Here's what I can tell you... and this is when I will be able to tell you more..." This way he was able to keep the trust and respect of the workers even though he was not giving them what they wanted.

THE INNER VOICES OF DOUBT

There is a natural descent as we enter the territory of Act 4; it happens in most Shakespeare histories and tragedies. If Henry started with his muse of fire and the call to imagination and inspiration, he now descends to the earthy mud of a battlefield, a far cry from the safe castles in which he began. As well as trying to deal with the doubts of his troops he will have to face his own fears, those inner demons that can either cause a leader to give up or, sometimes more dangerously, to make the wrong decision for the wrong reason.

As we embark on this inner journey why not hold a mirror up to Henry once more? Think about your own situation. What doubts will *you* meet in the "dark night"? How would you prepare to face your "Agincourt"?

ACT 4 • Scene 1

The dark night of the soul

THE STORY

The night before the battle is one of the longest scenes in the play. It begins with Henry, having returned from visiting the troops, talking privately with his brother:

> *Gloucester, 'tis true that we are in great danger;*
> *The greater therefore should our courage be.*

Sir Thomas Erpingham enters with a request that Henry accompany him to meet the other lords. Henry instead asks Sir Thomas for his cloak, takes off his crown and says:

> *Go with my brothers to my lords of England.*
> *I and my bosom must debate awhile,*
> *And then I would no other company.*

The King is alone for the first time since the story began, in disguise. He encounters several different groups of people on his walkabout; the first is Pistol (an old acquaintance from his tavern days), who, not recognizing him, gives his opinion of the King:

PISTOL	*The King's a bawcock and a heart-of-gold,*
	A lad of life, an imp of fame,
	Of parents good, of fist most valiant.
	I kiss his dirty shoe, and from heartstring
	I love the lovely bully. What is thy name?
HENRY	*Harry le roi.*
PISTOL	*Leroi? A Cornish name. Art thou of Cornish crew?*
HENRY	*No, I am a Welshman.*
PISTOL	*Know'st thou Llewellyn?*
HENRY	*Yes.*
PISTOL	*Tell him I'll knock his leek about his pate*
	Upon Saint David's day.

Pistol slinks off, no doubt about some devious business. Henry continues his walkabout, overhearing other conversations, until he comes upon three ordinary soldiers (John Bates, Alexander Court and Michael Williams) who seem fairly sure of what fate awaits them: "We see yonder the beginning of the day, but I think we shall never see the end of it." Henry joins them; the talk turns to responsibility:

BATES	*We know enough if we know we are the King's subjects.*
	If his cause be wrong, our obedience to the King wipes
	the crime of it out of us.
WILLIAMS	*But if the cause be not good, the King himself*
	hath a heavy reckoning to make...
	I am afeard there are few die well that die
	in a battle. Now, if these men do not die well, it will
	be a black matter for the King that led them to it.
HENRY	*So, if a son that is by his father sent about*
	merchandise do sinfully miscarry upon the sea, the
	imputation of his wickedness, by your rule, should be
	imposed upon his father, that sent him... But this
	is not so. The King is not bound to answer the particular
	endings of his soldiers, nor the father of his son, for they

purpose not their deaths when they purpose their services...
Every subject's duty is the King's, but every subject's soul
is his own.

They discuss whether the King will be ransomed, even though he has stated publicly that he will not. Williams insists: "He said so to make us fight cheerfully, but when our throats are cut he may be ransomed, and we ne'er the wiser." The King, even in disguise, finds it hard to take on board the soldier's cynicism and gets sucked first into an argument, then a challenge:

HENRY	*Your reproof is something too round. I should*
	be angry with you, if the time were convenient.
WILLIAMS	*Let it be a quarrel between us, if you live.*
HENRY	*I embrace it. Give me any gage of thine, and I will wear*
	it... Then if ever thou darest acknowledge
	it, I will make it my quarrel.

They exchange gloves and the soldiers leave. Henry is left alone again, with the weight of their concerns resting heavily on his shoulders. He speaks of the burden of leadership:

Upon the King.
"Let us our lives, our souls, our debts, our care-full wives,
Our children, and our sins, lay on the King."
We must bear all. O hard condition,
Twin-born with greatness: subject to the breath
Of every fool, whose sense no more can feel
But his own wringing. What infinite heartsease
Must kings neglect that private men enjoy?

Sir Thomas Erpingham comes in and reminds Henry: "My lord, your nobles, jealous of your absence, seek through your camp to find you." Henry says he will come. He gets on his knees and prays:

141

> *O God of battles, steel my soldiers' hearts.*
> *Possess them not with fear... Not today, O Lord,*
> *O not today, think not upon the fault*
> *My father made in compassing the crown.*

His brother, the Duke of Gloucester, now calls him. The King replies:

> *Ay. I know thy errand, I will go with thee.*
> *The day, my friends, and all things stay for me.*

THE INNER BATTLE

In the text there is no scripted battle at Agincourt. This is strange because we know that the audience of the time loved a good fight. The theatre was a place for all-round entertainment; acting, poetry, singing, dancing, music, clowning, humour and fights, especially big sword fights. But here at Agincourt – one of the most famous English victories in history – there are no scripted fights. It was only when we analyzed the text as a study of leadership that the reason for this became clear.

What Shakespeare shows us is Henry's battle to survive the "dark night", and he concentrates on the most important battle for a leader, the one inside. It is not your job to "go over the top" first, it is your job to look inside, check you are doing the right thing, and that you are the right person to be doing it. If you as a leader are able to go into the fears, doubts and uncertainties, and survive them, you will be able to reconnect to the vision that brought you into this now seemingly impossible-to-achieve mission in the first place. If you can do all that, you will be able to inspire the troops. This is winning the inner battle. What the troops then do externally is beyond your control. You have done what you can; the rest is up to others.

PRIVATE TRUTH

It is now some time after three o'clock in the morning. Henry has finally finished meeting the troops. After visible leadership and putting on the royal face, he makes time for private truth and revealing the human face: "Gloucester, 'tis true that we are in great danger..."

He finds a brother to whom he can speak his emotional reality. However brief the opportunity, the speaking of the private truth acts like a release valve, letting off steam. Of course, we have to choose our witness carefully. If you still have a Critic around the reply is likely to be "I told you so", which won't help much. Henry finds a brother whom he can trust absolutely. We often ask leaders if they have a "brother", "sister", mentor or close friend at the same sort of level in their organization to whom they can confide in this way. Not many do.

There is a subtle balance to be found between either staying everyone's friend and losing respect, or going it alone and ending up lonely, with no one to trust. It is here that the ability to build and sustain relationships will really pay off (the province of the Great Mother character); it takes time to nurture a friendship of this kind.

THE VALUE OF A MENTOR

If we do not have someone with whom we can share the private truth, it may fester inside of us, waiting to explode in some meeting or decision. If Henry did not have a brother to share the feeling of danger with, he might just start believing in the infallible "royal face" he showed the troops. If he allowed the Royal face to decide whether to fight, without checking the Human face, he could get into serious trouble. (The need to "unload" is becoming more culturally accepted with the rise of mentoring and coaching. It used to be frowned upon as "getting help", which translated into admitting weakness; now it is increasingly seen as a sign of mature responsibility.)

The "brother-mentor" is in a very different role from the strategy consultant, and you should take care not to confuse them. The consultant plans, strategizes and advises new ways of *doing*; the mentor initiates and facilitates new ways of *being*.

Henry has always had such mentor figures in his life. Falstaff introduced him to the real world outside the castle, allowing Henry to find himself as a young man, before becoming King. He asked the Lord Chief Justice to help him change his behaviour: "My voice shall sound as you do prompt my ear ... (to) your well-practised wise directions" (*Henry IV Part 2*, Act 5 Scene 2). And his brothers have been with him every step of his mission, providing support, appropriate challenge and a good ear.

APPROPRIATE SELFISHNESS

Henry is able to let off just enough steam with his brother that the next step becomes clear. He needs time alone. Dawn is approaching, beckoning in the day in which Henry will make the biggest decision of his life. Does he fight and risk 8,000 lives for the sake of his mission? Or does he face the logical reality (40,000 vs 8,000) and negotiate a ransom that will enable all to live? And in the midst of all this the nobles are getting understandably edgy. They are sending "e-mails" from all over the battlefield asking for a strategy meeting.

This is where Henry demonstrates appropriate selfishness. He holds his ground in the midst of the crisis. He knows that he has to sort himself out before he can sort out everyone else:

> *I and my bosom must debate awhile,*
> *And then I would no other company.*

There are many leaders I have worked with (and for) who can't do this. When things get tough, they are so identified with being "The Fixer" that they stay in the heat all the time. They never take a break to cool down and be with themselves. Eventually they often either burn out or make a serious error of judgement. If we allow ourselves to get pulled from pillar to post, from one crisis meeting to the next, how on earth can we really know what should happen, or even what we really think about the overall situation?

INAPPROPRIATE UNSELFISHNESS

I fell into this trap with a play I directed about 10 years ago. The story called for a number of involved technical set pieces and props, some of which had to appear dangerous to the audience but be absolutely safe for the actors. As we entered our technical rehearsals in the approach to opening night, the road became very rocky. As Director I was responsible for the outcome of the project. I had to manage nervous actors in genuine fear of injury, a backstage crew who had not got to grips with the physical requirements of the production, a producer determined to open on time, a set designer needing more time to complete his design, a lighting designer getting angry because set pieces kept moving position, a composer who couldn't complete his timed cues because we couldn't run scenes in proper time, and a fire inspector who wouldn't give us permission to use the set pieces until he had seen a complete run through of the play – which we couldn't do until most of the above had been completed. Oh, and we were scheduled to open in the West End in London in three weeks time.

It is fair to say that tensions were running high. I willingly stayed in the thick of it. I did not stop for a minute. It was my responsibility and – by heaven – I was going to be there and make sure everyone got what they needed. Except, of course, I never stopped to think what *I* needed, or, in fact, what the overall situation required. In the end, all of the short-term needs were met, by hook or by crook, *but...* the play did not work. When we could finally see the wood for the trees, it was not a wood worthy to go into a West End theatre; which was, of course, the stated intention of all concerned since the beginning of the project. So we had opened on time out of town, which had felt like winning a battle, but we never got to London, which meant we had lost the war. Big lesson – don't get so involved fixing others' concerns that you lose sight of your own.

TIME OUT

We run role plays to test people's ability to protect their own space in a crisis and often find them getting sucked into helping others, even though their specific task had been to make time for themselves. When we debrief they speak of "inner voices" saying "You'd better fix this for them, that's your job", or worse, "You don't really have the right to take time out – you are paid to know what to do right now".

In reality, the time out can be as simple as taking a five-minute break between meetings, or taking a walk around the block. Henry did not have time to go on a stress management course; he had about an hour to sort himself out. Being in or near nature helps; trees, water and natural surroundings seem to have a way of absorbing human tension – or at least of reminding us that it does not all have to be non-stop. The voice we need to hear at these times is the "inner coach" saying "Look, it's going to be tough out there. You are going to need all your faculties in good working order. You won't have them available if you keep fire-fighting for everyone else. Take some time and settle into what *you* want to do. And while you're there have a think about *why* you want to do it."

Henry takes a time out and wanders around the camp, in disguise. It is an irony of leadership that sometimes, in order to be ourselves, we may have to pretend *not* to be ourselves. Henry now needs to distance himself from the "royal face" in order to assess what is going on for him as a human being. It is a symbolic and important "de-roleing". Some of us are so invested in the role of Leader that we forget to drop it, and take off the crown.

LISTEN FIRST

Henry in disguise is also able to eavesdrop on others and listen to their realities. His time in the tavern has taught him the common touch; back in *Henry IV Part 1*, after drinking with tavern servants, he says; "they tell me I am a lad of mettle and when I am King of England I shall command all the good lads in Eastcheap"(Act 2 Scene 4). He knows how to talk and listen to people from all walks of life. Some modern leaders sit at the reception desk for a day to get the same view from the ground that Henry seeks here. After all, these are the people we are going to have to inspire to fight for our dream. If we don't know how they think, and what they are thinking, we won't know how to talk to them and what they need to hear.

OLD ACQUAINTANCES

The first person Henry encounters is Pistol, who does not recognize his old mate and speaks to him about the King:

> *The King's a bawcock and a heart-of-gold,*
> *A lad of life, an imp of fame,*
> *Of parents good, of fist most valiant.*
> *I kiss his dirty shoe, and from heartstring*
> *I love the lovely bully.*

Finally, I believe, here we have the vindication of Henry's earlier banishment of old dishonourable friends. Even though Pistol has (metaphorically) felt the weight of the King's foot and may label him a bully, there is love, respect and admiration in his description. He obviously trusts him as a leader and would follow him, willingly, unlike the stickler-for-discipline Llewellyn, whom he vows to insult: "Tell him I'll knock his leek about his pate upon Saint David's day."

Llewellyn would never hang out in a pub getting to know the people he will lead. A few moments later Henry overhears Llewellyn telling off his fellow captain Gower:

> *So! In the name of Jesu Christ, speak lower.*
> *If you would take the pains but to examine*
> *the ancient laws of the wars and the wars of*
> *Pompey the Great, you shall find, I warrant*
> *you, that there is no tiddle-taddle nor pibble-babble in*
> *Pompey's camp... If the enemy is an ass and a fool and a prating*
> *coxcomb, is it meet, think you, that we should also,*
> *look you, be an ass and a fool and a prating coxcomb?*

In your own conscience now?
GOWER   *I will speak lower.*
LLEWELLYN   *I pray you and beseech you that you will.*

He plays his Good King with a patronizing edge that people may obey but will never quite respect. He harps on about old rulebooks in a way that breeds begrudging acceptance, not the discretionary effort and willing followership needed to achieve miracles. Llewellyn may be loyal but he is not inspiring.

NEW ACQUAINTANCES

Henry walks on and meets a group of common soldiers, who reveal how his kingly ideas are received on the ground. The soldiers don't see any realistic possibility of surviving the battle and, like most troops the world over, they are quite prepared to blame the boss for their problems:

BATES   *We know enough if we know we are the King's subjects.*
If his cause be wrong, our obedience to the King wipes
the crime of it out of us.

(Which is the argument put forward by guards at torture sites the world over.)

WILLIAMS   *But if the cause be not good, the King himself*
hath a heavy reckoning to make…
I am afeard there are few die well that die
in a battle. Now, if these men do not die well, it will
be a black matter for the King that led them to it.

Henry is riled by their insistence that whatever happens to them it must be the King's fault. He attempts to explain the separate responsibilities of king and subject, leader and follower:

So, if a son that is by his father sent about
merchandise do sinfully miscarry upon the sea, the
imputation of his wickedness, by your rule, should be
imposed upon his father, that sent him… But this
is not so. The King is not bound to answer the particular
endings of his soldiers, nor the father of his son, for they
purpose not their deaths when they purpose their services…
Every subject's duty is the King's, but every subject's soul
is his own.

DISTINGUISHING BETWEEN DUTY AND SOUL

If we are going to step into positions in which we are going to affect the livelihoods of others, we had better get a grasp of this one. It is tough but, I believe, ultimately fair.

When people accept a job, whether in an office, a factory or the police force, there are certain risks that come with it. Providing the leader has taken all reasonable precautions, if some people get injured or killed it is not, personally, their fault. When the channel tunnel was planned it was almost certain that some injuries and fatalities would occur before completion – such risks come with the territory.

If you listen to the folk at the sharp end of such a project you will hear that it is the leaders that they hold responsible for their safety and lives. Henry is making an important distinction between the responsibility that a leader has, and that which he does *not* have. It is about intention. If a leader wishes to build a channel tunnel they may be aware that accidents will happen, but they do not intend them to happen and do their best to prevent them. Then if someone, aware of the risks involved in the job, does have an accident, that is deeply unfortunate and regretful. But it is not a responsibility on the leader's soul; "for they purpose not their deaths when they purpose their services." We start taking responsibility for the souls of our workforce at our peril.

In our seminar work with police leaders we ask them to role play a version of Henry listening to the troops, usually a conversation in the back of a transit van, waiting to enter a violent situation. Naturally, the lower ranks are complaining about the dangers that await them while the Commander, in disguise, tries to point out why it is necessary. It is another hard line to hold. If commanders are going to be able to inspire their troops they will need to know what they are thinking. But if they become too personally concerned for the safety of those people, they might start believing Williams's assertion that; "if these men do not die well, it will be a black matter for the King that led them to it." If leaders accept the responsibility others wish to project on them, they may hold back at the wrong moment or make the wrong decision for the wrong reason.

FUTURE CHALLENGE

Front line troops frequently think those above them are watching their own backs; that whatever a leader says, ultimately, they will look out for number one. As Williams says: "He (the King) said so (he would not be ransomed) to make us fight cheerfully, but when our throats are cut he may be ransomed, and we (will be none the) wiser." Henry's natural sense of honour is offended, and he instinctively defends himself: "If I live to see it, I will never trust his word after." Leaders find it hard – even in disguise – to listen to the troops' complaints without justifying their decisions. Williams pursues his train of thought to its natural conclusion: "Let it be a quarrel between us, if you live." Which Henry, now unused to being challenged as an equal, accepts; "I embrace it."

For all the folly of this exchange it also sows a valuable seed in Henry's mind. It is bravado, to be sure, but it has the effect of creating something to survive the battle for. Now, I grant you, it is a peculiar Warrior characteristic to be motivated to survive a battle so that you can fight with someone on your own side, *but*… it is the first time that any of these soldiers have considered the possibility of a future beyond the battle. Henry will draw on this chance exchange to inspire the troops later (in Act 4 Scene 3).

UNLOADING THE BURDEN

It is important to listen to the troops, and equally important not to be weighed down with the burden of their concerns, which at times of crisis are many. When the soldiers go off Henry is left with a heavy load:

> *Upon the King.*
> *"Let us our lives, our souls, our debts, our care-full wives,*
> *Our children, and our sins, lay on the King."*
> *We must bear all.*

The more worried people are, the more of their concerns they wish to pass on. This is sometimes referred to as the "monkey on the back" syndrome. The leader who bravely opens their door to all and sundry, often ends up with more than they had bargained for; remember Henry's words:

> *O hard condition,*
> *Twin-born with greatness: subject to the breath*
> *Of every fool, whose sense no more can feel*
> *But his own wringing.*

Everyone is eager to come into your office with some problem (their "monkey"), which is the only problem they can see. At the end of the day they feel better, but you may well have a menagerie of "monkeys" on your back:

> *What infinite heartsease*
> *Must kings neglect that private men enjoy?*

This is another one of those hard truths about leadership – along with the authority and the respect and the perks and privileges comes a heavy burden that can all too easily lead to sleepless nights.

THE NATURAL FLOW OF EMOTION

Henry's natural emotional intelligence allows him to express his feelings honestly. There is nothing else to be done with them at this point; but he does not need them weighing on his mind as he struggles to make the right decision. This expression is the key to a healthy emotional life, although it is not often realized in an organizational context. Feelings are like waves, they come and go. Some people refer to emotions as e-motions, energy in motion. What they need and want is to keep moving, like a wave that will build, peak and subside:

Many organizational cultures do not understand the simple human need to unload, especially the emotions that tend to be cast as "negative". And so, instead of expressing them, we repress them, much like building a dam in front of the wave:

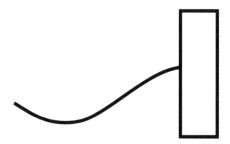

Except that they do not go away, these feelings we may wish we did not have, they wait until the next time and return with more force (water) behind them. The dam keeps them out, for a while, but eventually the water breaks through or over the dam:

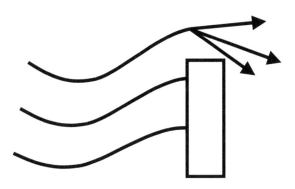

By this time the emotion has built up such a force that the result is often explosive and shocking. At which point we usually say: "Bloody hell! I knew these emotions were dangerous. I'd better build myself a bigger dam quick!"

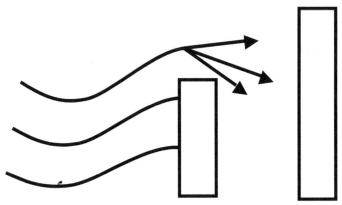

This "solution" leads to burn out and stress-related injury. What the emotion requires is an outlet. Simple expression. Henry gets his outlet through a good complain, what I call the "eternal leader's whinge".

In our seminars we often ask leaders to write down their burden of leadership in a letter. Most of these letters are remarkably similar. Many of the writers say they never usually allow themselves to express the burden, they keep it locked up. But locked up it will eat away from the inside. Better out than in, as they say. And better out in private, on your own terms, than a public explosion that affects others.

FACING THE SHADOW

The key to surviving the "dark night" is to go into it, rather than avoid it. To accept that if your project is important it *will* enter a stage when it appears impossible to achieve. That is the real test of leadership, and you will never get the time you want to meet the test. What's more, the pressure around you will not stop simply because you have decided to face the dark night. As Sir Thomas Erpingham proves when he tracks Henry down to remind him: "My lord, your nobles, jealous of your absence, seek through your camp to find you." Henry has taken his time out, but it is still the morning before the battle. He has one more need to fulfil before he returns to the fray. He prays:

> *Not today, O Lord,*
> *O not today, think not upon the fault*
> *My father made in compassing the crown.*

Many of us may not have anyone we wish to pray to, but that does not negate the psychological effect of what Henry does here. I call it "facing the shadow". Looking deep within to find the piece of you that might just trip yourself up in a crisis, and acknowledging it. It is a self-aware early warning system. Henry prays that the faults he and his family have made in the past do not come home to roost on him and his soldiers today. His father took the throne from Richard II and was at least partly responsible for his death. Henry has grown up fighting civil wars and the Warrior is his favourite role.

Now is the time to check that we are not bringing the "inner traitors" with us to "Agincourt". For Henry, it means facing the potentially addicted Warrior fair and square. It is as if he were saying; "I do not wish to be ruled by you today. Not by the one who never gives up, no matter what the cost, who never admits defeat because it would look weak. That is not the right character to make this decision today".

Other "inner traitors" linked to other characters would be different. The Negative Great Mother might want to give in to protect life and limb, no matter the ultimate cost. The Negative Good King might want more analysis of the situation and wait to make a purely logical decision. The Negative Medicine Woman might set up a brainstorming meeting to find creative alternative solutions. We all have our own version of one or more of these inner figures. It is important to meet them and face them down before we come out of the dark night.

CORE VALUES

By this time Henry has stripped away roles and projections. Like peeling layers from an onion, he is down to his core – and therefore can reconnect to his core values. These are what inspired his vision in the first place, but this time it is actually a deeper connection, because it is one he has found in the darkness, and by himself.

There is a natural resistance to entering the dark night, but it is the only real proving ground for the tough decisions we will have to make in our lives. David Whyte talks about this in his poem *Sweet Darkness*:

SWEET DARKNESS

When your eyes are tired
the world is tired also.

When your vision has gone
no part of the world can find you.

Time to go into the dark
where the night has eyes
to recognize its own.

There you can be sure
you are not beyond love.

The dark will be your womb
tonight.

The night will give you a horizon
further than you can see.

You must learn one thing.
The world was made to be free in.

Give up all the other worlds
except the one to which you belong.

Sometimes it takes darkness and the sweet
confinement of your aloneness
to learn

anything or anyone
that does not bring you alive

is too small for you.

This is the final check. Does the vision still "bring you alive"? Is it too small, or too big for you? Is this the right way to realize your vision? Are you the right person to lead these people into this situation right now?

And, of course, some leaders don't make it through. Recently the Manager of the England football team resigned unexpectedly, in the middle of a campaign. In his "dark night" he saw that he was not the right person. The Chief Executive of Coca Cola UK recently stepped down to spend more time with her family, she had got to a level where she felt the company wanted all of her life, and she simply was not prepared to give it. It was not the right mission.

There is no right or wrong, there is only what is right or wrong for you. If the inner confirmation is there *after* facing the dark night, you have earned the right to fight for it. Now Henry is ready to meet his nobles and his troops:

Ay. I know thy errand, I will go with thee.
The day, my friends, and all things stay for me.

ACT 4 • Scene 2

Hot air

THE STORY

The French lords are armed and ready for the battle. The Lord Constable rallies them together:

> *To horse, you gallant princes, straight to horse!*
> *Do but behold yon poor and starvèd band,*
> *And your fair show shall suck away their souls,*
> *Leaving them but the shells and husks of men.*
> *There is not work enough for all our hands,*
> *Let us but blow on them...*
> *The vapour of our valour will o'erturn them...*
> > *'Tis positive, lords,*
> *That our superfluous lackeys and our peasants,*
> *Were enough to purge this field of such a foe...*
> *What's to say? A very little little let us do*
> *And all is done. Then let the trumpets sound*
> *For our approach shall so much dare the field*
> *That England shall couch down in fear and yield.*

COMMENT

The long night has done nothing to dampen the supreme confidence of the French. Their attitude assumes, among other things, that they will win because they are better dressed (which some assert was IBM's first response to Microsoft!) That if they talk themselves up enough, "blowing" on the enemy with valiant words will be sufficient to overturn them (Saddam Hussein to George Bush Snr). That their assistants could do the job for them (Sir Alex Ferguson and Manchester United with the Worthington Cup) and that the very sound of the approaching attack will cause a panicked surrender (British Prime Minister Tony Blair trying to dissuade Ken Livingstone from running for Mayor of London). And they say Pride come before a... what was it now?

ACT 4 • Scene 3

Inspiring the troops

THE STORY

The nobles wait for Henry in his tent:

GLOUCESTER   *Where is the King?*
BEDFORD   *The King himself is rode to view their battle.*
EXETER   *Of fighting men they have full threescore thousand.*
     There's five to one. Besides, they all are fresh.
WESTMORELAND *'Tis a fearful odds... O that we now had here*
     But one ten thousand of those men in England
     That do no work today.

The King has come in unseen and overheard the request; he speaks:

> *What's he that wishes so?*
> *My cousin, Westmoreland? No, my fair cousin.*
> *If we are marked to die, we are enough*
> *To do our country loss; and if to live,*
> *The fewer men, the greater share of honour.*
> *God's will, I pray thee wish not one man more.*
> *By Jove, I am not covetous for gold,*
> *It yearns me not if men my garments wear;*
> *Such outward things dwell not in my desires.*
> *But if it be a sin to covet honour*

I am the most offending soul alive.
No, faith, my coz, wish not a man from England.
Rather proclaim it presently through my host
That he which hath no stomach to this fight,
Let him depart. His passport shall be made
And crowns for convoy put into his purse.
We would not die in that man's company
That fears his fellowship to die with us.
This day is called the Feast of Crispian.
He that outlives this day and comes safe home
Will stand a-tiptoe when this day is named
And rouse him at the name of Crispian.
He that shall see this day and live old age
Will yearly on the vigil feast his neighbours
And say, "Tomorrow is Saint Crispian."
Then will he strip his sleeve and show his scars
And say, "These wounds I had on Crispin's day."
Old men forget; yet all shall be forgot,
But he'll remember, with advantages,
What feats he did that day. Then shall our names,
Familiar in his mouth as household words…
Be in their flowing cups freshly remembered.
This story shall the good man teach his son,
And Crispin Crispian shall ne'er go by
From this day to the ending of the world
But we in it shall be rememberèd,
We few, we happy few, we band of brothers.
For he today that sheds his blood with me
Shall be my brother; be he ne'er so vile,
This day shall gentle his condition.
And gentlemen in England now abed
Shall think themselves accursed they were not here,
And hold their manhoods cheap whiles any speaks
That fought with us upon Saint Crispin's day.

The Earl of Salisbury comes in to tell Henry the French are ready to attack:

HENRY	*All things are ready if our minds be so.*
WESTMORELAND	*Perish the man whose mind is backward now.*
HENRY	*Thou dost not wish more help from England, coz?*
WESTMORELAND	*God's will, my liege, would you and I alone,*
	Without more help, could fight this royal battle.
HENRY	*Why now thou hast unwished five thousand men,*
	Which likes me better than to wish us one. —
	You know your places. God be with you all.

The French Herald Montjoy enters to ask if Henry will now negotiate his ransom before his "most assurèd overthrow" and take pity on his soldiers' souls that they may retreat "From off these fields where, wretches, their poor bodies must lie and fester."

But Henry has made up his mind:

HENRY	*Come thou no more for ransom, gentle herald.*
	They shall have none, I swear, but these my joints—
	Which if they have as I will leave 'em them,
	Shall yield them little. Tell the Constable.
MONTJOY	*I shall, King Harry. And so fare thee well.*
	Thou never shalt hear herald any more.
HENRY	(aside) *I fear thou wilt once more come for a ransom.*

WHAT'S IN IT FOR ME?

While Henry has been on his walkabout the nobles have been busy calculating the odds. Now they publicly wish for more troops. (Funny that, senior managers wanting more resources!) Henry faces a different challenge to the one at Harfleur; at Harfleur they had to achieve the first foothold, now they need to be inspired to fight against the odds. There are defining moments in all our lives and in all the roles we choose to play; this is the moment which sets Henry among the ranks of truly inspirational leaders. He starts, as he will finish, by addressing the request for more troops:

> *No, my fair cousin.*
> *If we are marked to die, we are enough*
> *To do our country loss; and if to live,*
> *The fewer men, the greater share of honour.*

Having survived his "dark night", he knows why he is here – because he believes it is the right and honourable place to be – and what he is here for:

> *By Jove, I am not covetous for gold,*
> *It yearns me not if men my garments wear;*
> *Such outward things dwell not in my desires.*
> *But if it be a sin to covet honour*
> *I am the most offending soul alive.*

Sometimes, in order to follow you into a seriously tough battle, your people need to know why *you* are doing it. What gets you out of bed in the morning for this fight – besides the gold, the salary or the prospective bonus? Why do you believe this is an honourable cause, the right path to be pursuing? The "outward things" won't help here; most of your people would be able to get similar "outward things" from other leaders, other organizations. It is not *what* you can offer them, but *who* is leading them that they need to know. And if you have not gone through the "dark night" you may not know the answer.

LESS IS MORE

Henry continues, making what many assume to be a foolhardy offer:

> *No, faith, my coz, wish not a man from England.*
> *Rather proclaim it presently through my host*

> *That he which hath no stomach to this fight,*
> *Let him depart. His passport shall be made*
> *And crowns for convoy put into his purse.*
> *We would not die in that man's company*
> *That fears his fellowship to die with us.*

If everyone stuck their hand up and said "Yes please, I'll take the money and run", Henry would, technically speaking, be stuffed. If the majority of people have only followed him because it was a job, something to do, something to bring in a daily crust, he wouldn't have many left. But Henry has sown the seeds of inspiration well. He encouraged others to buy in to the mission before it started, connected the mission to a line of service ("Harry, England and Saint George!"), and has motivated them over all obstacles so far. They'll stay.

There is also a peculiar wisdom in the offer. I can think of several big projects I have been involved in, which some people walked out of, and those remaining achieved twice as much in half the time. By cutting away the dead wood you can sometimes do more with less. Better to have a few inspired "brothers" than a load of resentful followers.

THE GIFT OF A FUTURE

Now Henry draws an image from the future, and gives his listeners a glimpse of life beyond the battle. He does not talk about the details of the fight to come and what he expects of them, he talks about their retirement!

> *This day is called the Feast of Crispian.*
> *He that outlives this day and comes safe home*
> *Will stand a-tiptoe when this day is named*
> *And rouse him at the name of Crispian.*
> *He that shall see this day and live t' old age*
> *Will yearly on the vigil feast his neighbours*
> *And say, "Tomorrow is Saint Crispian."*

Then will he strip his sleeve and show his scars
And say, "These wounds I had on Crispin's day."
Old men forget; yet all shall be forgot,
But he'll remember, with advantages,
What feats he did that day. Then shall our names,
Familiar in his mouth as household words...
Be in their flowing cups freshly remembered.
This story shall the good man teach his son,
And Crispin Crispian shall ne'er go by
From this day to the ending of the world
But we in it shall be rememberèd.

This, to me, is the core of the speech. Henry offers the gift of a future to a group who, up till this moment, has not seen any future; they have been waiting to die. Nor does he make any false promises. He does not say; "I think most of us will make it", he says that any one who makes it will remember this day and his comrades, forever. When he says *"He that outlives this day..."* everyone listening thinks "That could be me. I could be the one. I'll have a drink for you lot, promise."

In the moment Henry paints this picture of the future those listening will start to see it, and when they do, it becomes a possible reality for them. They follow Henry's imagination to see themselves as old men on the anniversary of the battle, in the pub, having a drink and toasting their mates. And then, from the vantage point of this imagined future, Henry gets them all to look back – *on a battle that they have not even fought yet* – as though it were in the past. In their imaginations they have already moved beyond the ugly reality of the present to a happy imagined future from which they can reflect on their glorious struggle. Now they have something to fight for. Survival and honour.

"THE FEW"

Lastly, Henry turns the outrageous odds into an inspiring challenge:

We few, we happy few, we band of brothers.
For he today that sheds his blood with me
Shall be my brother; be he ne'er so vile,
This day shall gentle his condition.

He glories in the inequality of numbers, calling out a sense of honour in the underdog. He not only includes himself in the battle with them, he also makes a virtue out of them shedding blood together which, he promises, will bind them together in a bond of brotherhood. This is an extraordinary offer of equality, particularly as in Elizabethan times the monarch was believed to be touched by the divine. Even today a respected leader who transmits the sense that others can be equal to him or her will inspire:

And gentlemen in England now abed
Shall think themselves accursed they were not here,
And hold their manhoods cheap whiles any speaks
That fought with us upon Saint Crispin's day.

The final reversal – it will not be us wishing others were here, it will be those others wishing they had been here, to share in the glory of the struggle. It is as if Henry were saying: "Come on guys, if we had 100,000 here it wouldn't be a real achievement. You'd forget about it in a few years. But if we can win, with 8,000, now that would be one to remember." He makes a blessing out of their complaint, and reawakens the part in all his listeners that wants to be extraordinary, that yearns to be remembered for a great achievement.

When Henry hears the French are preparing to fight he says "All things are ready if our minds be so" (sports/performance psychologists would agree). And finally Westmoreland, he who wanted more troops, proves that Henry has indeed "readied" the minds of others:

God's will, my liege, would you and I alone,
Without more help, could fight this royal battle.

As a whole, this is one of the most inspiring speeches in English literature, and it rarely fails to stir up not only the troops on stage, but the audience as well. The impact of this speech was a key factor in Winston Churchill encouraging my father to make his film of *Henry V* during the Second World War, to build morale for the Normandy landings. The story of a successful invasion of France might just ready some more modern minds. Churchill himself memorably drew from Henry's image of "the happy few" when speaking of the "Battle of Britain":

> The gratitude of every home in our island, in our Empire, and indeed throughout the world, except in the abodes of the guilty, goes out to the British airmen who, undaunted by odds, unwearied by their constant challenge and mortal danger, are turning the tide of world war by their prowess and by their devotion. *Never in the field of human conflict was so much owed by so many to so few.*
>
> (From Churchill's speech to the House of Commons, 20 August 1940)

HARDENING THE RESOLVE

By the time Montjoy arrives with another offer of ransom, it is too late. All the Herald succeeds in doing is giving the King one more chance to answer Williams and any other soldier that doubts his resolve:

> *Come thou no more for ransom, gentle herald.*
> *They shall have none, I swear, but these my joints—*
> *Which if they have as I will leave 'em them,*
> *Shall yield them little.*

This is not a leader who will risk his people and then look to save himself. People appreciate hearing such loyalty. I recently coached a director in the National Health Service to risk sharing the private loyalty he felt for his staff with them in public. He told me afterwards he had never received such grateful comments from staff before, nor had he ever thought it necessary to let them know how much he wanted to protect them and how willing he was to fight for them.

A STING IN THE TAIL

After all this – Harfleur, the "dark night", inspiring his troops, publicly refusing to surrender – the private fears remain, just below the surface. As the Herald Montjoy leaves, Shakespeare has Henry mutter under his breath, to himself: "I fear thou wilt once more come for a ransom". Which would only happen if the English were near defeat. You can never be sure that any given course of action will succeed, even if you believe it is the right way to go.

ACT 4 • Scene 4

A hostage for fortune

THE STORY

Pistol and the Boy capture a French soldier, Le Fer. Pistol, who may have been listening to Montjoy, gives his prisoner a similar choice: "Thou diest, on point of (sword), except, O Seigneur, thou do give to me egregious ransom." The Boy interprets Monsieur Le Fer's offer: "He prays you to save his life... and for his ransom he will give you two hundred crowns." To which Pistol replies: "Tell him, my fury shall abate, and I the crowns will take." Pistol and his captive go off, leaving the Boy to reflect:

> *I did never know so full a voice issue from so empty a*
> *heart. Bardolph and Nym are both hanged, and so would*
> *this be, if he steal anything adventurously. I must stay with*
> *the lackeys with the luggage of our camp. The French*
> *might have a good prey of us, if he knew of it, for there*
> *is none to guard it but boys.*

COMMENT

Once again Shakespeare undercuts honourable talk with dishonourable actions. We leave Henry and his nobles to find Pistol making a quick buck. It is another example of Shakespeare's inclusivity, always prepared to come down to earth after flights into fiery inspiration.

We are reminded that however honourable our intentions there will always be some who follow us only for the gold, for what's in it for them. The gold diggers who live for their appetites may have a full stomach but, like Pistol, they will usually have an "empty heart" to go with it. Those with integrity never follow them willingly, only through coercion or necessity. Some will never take a mission or a vision to heart. Maybe we shouldn't always take ourselves too seriously either.

We hear, by the by, that Nym has joined Bardolph on the scaffold, obviously unable to resist the temptation to steal – even after witnessing the execution of his friend – and that Pistol is in danger of joining them.

Finally, we hear that the Boy is off to guard the luggage, and could become an easy prey for the French...

ACT 4 • Scene 5

Confounding the French

THE STORY

The French lords are not doing as well as they expected. In fact, they are being soundly beaten:

DAUPHIN	*Mort de ma vie! All is confounded, all.*
ORLEANS	*We are enough yet living in the field*
	To smother up the English in our throngs,
	If any order might be thought upon.
DAUPHIN	*The devil take order. Once more back again!*

CONSTABLE   *Disorder that hath spoiled us friend us now.*
            Let us on heaps go offer up our lives.
DAUPHIN   *I'll to the throng.*
            Let life be short, else shame will be too long.

FROM ORDER TO CHAOS – HENRY'S BATTLE PLAN

The over-confident bubble has burst. Chaos has replaced the expectation of quick victory. The strategy that Henry historically used to get the French into this mess was a mixture of luck, improvization, good judgement and bad weather. It is a strategy still taught at Sandhurst military college. The diagram below is a much simplified outline.

During the march from Harfleur the French had sent mounted raiding parties to pick off a few of the walking English. Henry therefore ordered all his men to cut down a six-foot branch from a tree, sharpen it to a

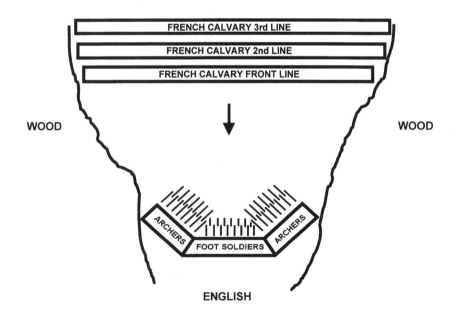

Henry's Battle Plan

HILL

FRENCH CALVARY 3rd LINE

FRENCH CALVARY 2nd LINE

FRENCH CALVARY FRONT LINE

WOOD   WOOD

ARCHERS

ARCHERS

FOOT SOLDIERS

ENGLISH

point at both ends and carry it on the march. When a raiding party appeared they could stick their branch into the ground, stand behind it and be protected. (Imagine the complaints from the exhausted men on being ordered to carry extra weight.) So at Agincourt, Henry had approximately 8,000 sharpened branches at his disposal, which he ordered to be stuck firmly in the ground in front of his troops.

The French had placed themselves on top of the hill to get what they thought would be the advantage. The English were waiting at the bottom with longbow men on each flank. It had been raining all night and the bottom of the hill in front of the English troops was thick with mud.

So much for the weather, the strategy and the improvization. The luck arrived in the attitude of the French, who had been set in three ranks of horsemen at the top of the hill. As the play reveals their only concern was that there would not be enough work for them to do. As a result, when the order was given for the front rank of horses to attack, those behind pushed in to join what they feared would be their only chance of glory.

Now geography and topography conspired against them. The open space between the wooded land on either side of the hill narrowed as it got closer to the bottom. So, as the (much larger than planned) first attack descended they began to drift into the middle from both sides. It got to the point where the horses were so close together that their riders were unable to lift their arms to raise their weapons or shields. Add to this volleys of armour-piercing longbows raining down, causing horses to fall and those behind to trip over them, and you have the beginning of chaos. The final straw was, of course, the sharpened wooden staves. When the unfortunate French did get to the bottom of the hill their steeds simply ran onto the sticks. The mud made it impossible to stop or turn around in heavy armour, so those behind simply ran into the back of those stuck in front. Still unable to lift an arm to defend themselves the French were totally helpless. The English picked up clubs, walked from horseback to horseback, and knocked the French unconscious.

In the simplest terms, this is the situation the French lords found themselves in. "All is confounded". Indeed.

Henry's ability to improvize with the sticks was to prove a major turning point. It is the type of on the spot thinking more associated with tavern than castle. He was also patient. Historically, the battle lines formed around eight in the morning and the French waited at the top of the hill, trying to force the English to attack them. Henry was prepared to outwait them behind his sticks at the bottom. By midday the French had become impatient and decided to attack downhill.

The French had also decided that the long ranged crossbow was not an honourable weapon, unlike their crossbows, which they thought more civilized. They were so outraged by Henry's decision to employ the crossbow men that they threatened to cut off the bow fingers of any they captured. Later, when the French prisoners were marched past, the crossbow men took delight in waving their bow fingers at the French; the origin of the triumphant "V" sign.

ACT 4 • Scene 6

Killing the prisoners

THE STORY

Henry enters with some of his men and some of their prisoners. He tells his men that they have done well, but they must keep fighting for the French are still on the field. The Duke of Exeter enters and speaks to Henry of the death of two lords, the Duke of York and the Earl of Suffolk. Both men are moved by the tale, until an alarum sounds, signifying a new French attack. Henry has to think quickly, on his feet:

> *But hark, what new alarum is this same?*
> *The French have reinforced their scattered men.*
> *Then every soldier kill his prisoners.*
> *Give the word through.*

THE HARDEST CHOICE

This decision is the one that has outlived Henry more than any other. Military strategists and moral philosophers down the centuries have debated it. Does a leader ever have the right to kill their prisoners? Let's have a look at the situation (see diagram below).

The English have defeated the first charge of the French and have been collecting prisoners behind their lines. The French prisoners now outnumber their guards. Half of the English are starting to disarm and de-armour their prisoners when the French trumpet sounds the next attack.

Put yourself in Henry's shoes for a moment. There is at least 20,000 French horse at the top of the hill, waiting to charge; there are approximately 5,000 French prisoners behind your lines currently occupying about 4,000 of your total of 8,000 troops. What would you do?

The Battlefield

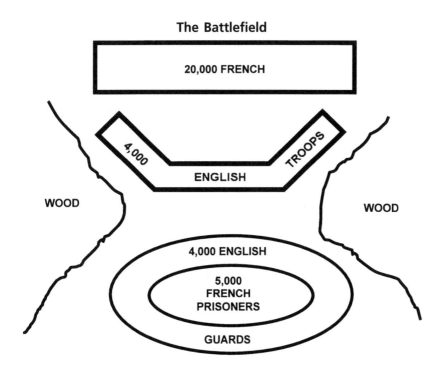

Henry opts for the apparently brutal decision of killing the prisoners. If he had not done so, he risked his small force being caught in the middle and annihilated. In a sense, it is a dilemma not unlike the one faced by the American High Command towards the end of the Second World War when they dropped the atom bombs on Japan; the alternative being to engage their troops in hand-to-hand combat for months through the Pacific Islands. It was estimated that the cost of such an operation was likely to be nearly a million American casualties. The decision to drop the bombs was partly based on the probability of this saving 1,000,000 American lives. Henry's decision was similarly based on the probability of saving 8,000 English lives.

LEADING MAY NOT BE GOOD FOR YOU...

No one would ever wish to have to make this kind of decision. But those who step into leadership will be more likely than others to face this kind of harsh reality (if not on such an horrendous scale).

Early on in our *Henry V* seminars I worked with Sean, a senior director from a major beverage company in Ireland. He was an ambitious and talented leader on his way up the ranks who had been tasked with restructuring the organization in the wake of a recent take-over. At a certain point it became clear that a whole raft of middle management would not survive the transition and it fell to Sean to tell them. His job, for six weeks straight, would be to see these 600 people, one by one, and let them know they were surplus to requirements. He started confidently enough on week one, at Monday morning, nine o'clock. By Friday at five he was a wreck. He had had everything bar the kitchen sink thrown at him. Papers, chairs, insults, tears, screams of anger, children's education, family holidays – you name it he had faced it during that week. He did not know how he could possibly survive the next five weeks, or even if he wanted to.

That weekend he went through his own "dark night". He went for long walks and eventually realized that he did, actually, believe in what was being done and why. He knew, in his bones, that it was necessary, and that the organization would not survive if it kept on carrying the weight of the

600. It felt a lot like killing prisoners. Horrible but necessary. He also saw that he was the only person to do it, it was his responsibility.

By Monday morning he was ready to continue, but with a subtle but important difference. When it came time to get dressed he stood in front of a mirror and as he put on his company tie he thought to himself; "OK, you are now becoming the 'Company Killer'. You won't enjoy it, but it is the right thing to do and there is no one else to do it". And off he went to work, with this invisible protection around him. He sat through the hard day's work, and while he did not necessarily get anything less thrown at him, he did not take it so personally. Some part of him recognized that he was representing a larger entity, and attempting to serve the many more people who would stay and hopefully prosper in the company for a long time to come. Equally important, when he got home he went back to the mirror, took off the tie and thought: "You are no longer the 'Company Killer'. Now you can be Sean again."

Every so often a leader will be put in the position of apparently having to make innocent people suffer, either for survival, or for the sake of the vision, or just to please the shareholders. It is up to you to figure out if it is the right thing to do and if you, personally, can cope with it. I do not advocate a depersonalized approach to work; but occasionally we need to protect ourselves in order to do the hard things that have to be done, and not go mad.

ACT 4 • Scene 7

The price of victory

THE STORY

Llewellyn enters with Gower, furious that the French have raided the luggage tents and killed all the boys. Gower exclaims this is why "the King most worthily hath caused every soldier to cut his prisoner's throat, O 'tis a gallant King."

Henry enters, shouting: "I was not angry since I came to France until this instant." He is followed by Montjoy, the French Herald, who has a request:

> *O give us leave, great King,*
> *To view the field in safety, and dispose*
> *Of our dead.*

HENRY   *I tell thee truly, herald,*
I know not if the day be ours or no...

MONTJOY   *The day is yours.*

HENRY   *Praisèd be God, and not our strength, for it.*

Henry names it the battle of Agincourt and Llewellyn takes the opportunity to launch into a lengthy conversation with the King. He is only interrupted when Henry spots Williams, who has survived the battle and is now looking for the "rascal" that "swaggered with me last night" to whom he owes "a box on the ear".

With a little cunning deception, Henry manages to get Llewellyn to wear Williams's glove on his behalf and receive his box on the ear. When Llewellyn demands Williams be hung as a traitor Henry reveals himself as the original challenger, forgives Williams and fills his glove with gold crowns.

An English herald enters and hands Henry the lists of the dead:

HENRY   *This note doth tell me of ten thousand French*
That in the field lie slain...
The number of our English dead...
Edward the Duke of York, the Earl of Suffolk,
Sir Richard Keighley, Davy Gam Esquire;
None else of name, and of all other men
But five-and-twenty. O God, thy arm was here,
And not to us, but to thy arm alone
Ascribe we all...
Come, go we in procession to the village,

And be it death proclaimèd through our host
To boast of this, or take that praise from God
Which is His only...

THE DEATH OF INNOCENCE

There comes a moment in all leaders' lives when they lose their innocence. We like to think that if the mission is "right" and our integrity intact then we can get through the worst struggles and hardest challenges without such loss.

Whatever remained of Henry's innocence as a leader has died with the prisoners. And immediately we hear news of the death of the Boy, the symbol of innocence in the play. It is not an accident. The law of cause and effect has been operating; Henry and his troops have killed unarmed prisoners to survive, but there is a price to pay. Now he hears that the unarmed English boys are dead.

Henry cannot help but feel partly responsible for this event. When he says "I was not angry since I came to France until this instant", he is not just angry with the French, but with himself, and with his God, who back when the traitors were discovered seemed to have promised him "a fair and lucky war". At this moment he feels neither. His faith is only revived when Montjoy tells him he has won the day: "Praisèd be God, and not our strength, for it." His anger turns to praise, relief and wonder.

Sometimes hard decisions win the day, but there is usually a price to be paid.

Henry has been well and truly "blooded" as a leader.

HENRY THE TRICKSTER-TEACHER

Following the announcement of victory and preceding the lists of the dead, there is a fascinating interaction between Henry, the loyal and pompous Llewellyn, and the forthright soldier Williams. Despite the historic and miraculous victory that Henry has achieved he does not devote his attention to celebrating with his nobles, but to a complicated piece of man management involving a captain and a common soldier.

When Williams appears looking for his challenger from the previous night, Henry could, of course, simply reveal himself and have Williams punished for publicly doubting the King's word. But instead he moves into Medicine Woman mode. He uses disguise, deception and creative imagination to create an opportunity for development that could transform both Williams and Llewellyn. He has seen the potential of both and witnessed at first hand the limiting attitudes that may block that potential. Williams is honest but cynical, Llewellyn loyal but patronizing; neither is yet able to communicate with, or manage, others effectively.

Henry calls Williams over and gets him to tell the story behind the challenge, then asks Llewellyn if the soldier should keep his oath to fetch his challenger a "box on the ear" even if he were "a gentleman of great sort". Llewellyn insists that Williams must carry out his oath or be "a craven and a villain else. If he be perjured, see you now, his reputation is an arrant villain." There is no hint of uncertainty in Llewellyn's mind; no grey areas, only black and white, right and wrong.

When Williams is safely out of earshot Henry pulls out the glove he gave him the night before and hands it to Llewellyn, pretending it belongs to an enemy, the Duke of Alencon, and that Llewellyn should apprehend anyone who challenges it. Llewellyn suspects nothing and promises to carry out his duty. As soon as Williams sees the glove he challenges it and hits Llewellyn. The King and his brothers intervene and arrest Williams before any real damage is done. As the truth is revealed Llewellyn demands Williams be hanged as a traitor, noticeably forgetting his own prescriptive advice of a few moments previously that Williams must fight, no matter what. He then stands by, astounded, as Henry not only forgives Williams, but rewards him with a glove full of gold crowns. The King then insists that Llewellyn make peace with Williams.

Henry, in his new role of trickster-teacher, knows that sometimes you have to trick people into the learning they need (ask your HR Director), and a lecture is never as powerful as an experience. Symbolically, at that time, a glove was known to represent faith, loyalty and trust – the equivalent of giving someone your hand. Henry cunningly facilitates a situation where Williams will experience a lesson in trust and Llewellyn a lesson about blind loyalty.

BUILDING A POSITIVE CYCLE OF TRUST

Williams learns that sometimes it is better to keep cynical opinions to oneself, particularly when those opinions cast doubt on the integrity of a leader who has given people no reason to doubt him. Williams has interpreted the King's word (that he will not be ransomed) as a political ploy: "He said so to make us fight cheerfully, but when our throats are cut he may be ransomed, and we ne'er the wiser."

But as we have seen, an inspired leader is in a line of service. He would not ask others to make sacrifices for a mission he would not be willing to make sacrifices for himself.

If all the straightforward honest workers/soldiers like Williams were habitually to judge their leaders as cynical and political, they would undermine the trust those leaders need from their troops – especially when faced with an Agincourt. If Williams were to spread his negative message throughout the camp a lot of soldiers might lose heart, and be less inspired to fight, and therefore less likely to win. The magic of "a little touch of Harry in the night" can be lost with an unhealthy dose of cynicism at dawn!

Williams's arrest shocks him into being more careful with his opinions in future: "Your majesty came not as yourself... therefore I made no offence, I beseech your Highness pardon me". He is then rewarded by Henry, who knows it was a natural (though unhelpful) response, not a premeditated attempt to undermine him: "Uncle Exeter, fill this glove with crowns... Keep it fellow and wear it for an honour in thy cap".

Treating others as trustworthy will build a positive cycle of trust around you, treating them an untrustworthy will create a negative spiral. It particularly affects discretionary effort. If I act as if I trust others, it will make no difference to those who are untrustworthy (they put in the same effort with or without trust), but I will harness the discretionary effort of the trustworthy (who need reciprocal trust to put in their best effort). If I use the inevitable presence of a few untrustworthy folk to make me distrust everyone, it still makes no difference to the effort of the untrustworthy, but I lose the discretionary effort of the trustworthy which, during the hard times, I cannot afford to do.

SEEING THE INDIVIDUAL

Llewellyn is also changed by this encounter. Throughout the story he has taken things at face value (thinking Pistol "as valiant a man as Mark Antony" because Pistol talks himself up) and placed a blind loyalty in doing things by the book, according to "the laws of the wars". He insists Williams must keep his word no matter how high in rank his challenger, then when Williams does so, Llewellyn demands he be hanged as a traitor. He moves from his received notion of the code of honour to a received notion of treachery without seeking to understand the human situation.

Henry teaches Llewellyn by example; he models the human face of leadership. The King changes his attitude to Williams, not by referring to a different book, but by talking to the human being in front of him. He starts off seeing him as an offending soldier, but ends up seeing an honest man who has made a natural mistake, and even rewards him. It is as if he were saying to Llewellyn "Look, this man is not just a number, to be dealt with by the book, but an individual. As a leader you have a responsibility to see the individuals you lead. Sometimes you have to drop the rules and look at the human being."

In this scene we witness Henry's belief in human potential. As a leader he does not merely seek to use people to serve his ends, he seeks to improve them, and to create situations where they can improve themselves. Again, his days in the tavern pay off; his ability to play act, role play and create opportunities as they emerge in front of him was learnt from Falstaff and the gang, not from the nobles. There is no right place to learn these kinds of leadership skills, but Henry brings all his past experience with him and is not afraid to use it. This interaction does not require logical analysis, but creativity and spontaneous opportunity – the character of the Medicine Woman.

MODESTY IN VICTORY

The miraculous victory at Agincourt is reinforced when we hear the lists of the dead; 10,000 French, 25 English. Henry is truly humbled and insists that no one "boast of this, or take that praise from God, which is His only".

If we are in a true line of service we do not seek credit or applause. Even without the trust in God that sustains Henry, we can all sense some times when there is a "flow" around us, when it does not feel like *we* are doing it, but rather that *"it"* is happening. Many creative artists feel as if they themselves are an instrument through which a theme or bigger story is being played out.

> My father told me a story of a tour of *Richard III* he did in 1945 to entertain the troops on the continent after D-day. He was on a hectic schedule doing one night in a city, travelling overnight, setting up in the next city, playing and going on. After a few weeks he was shattered. He got into his dressing room one night in Hamburg and did not know how he would get through the play. At the half-hour call a stage manager came in and switched on a tannoy system, which meant he was able to hear the audience gathering out front. As he heard the anticipation in the troops' buzzy talk he felt a new energy enter him, he did not know from where. He went out and gave the best performance of his life, and when he got back to the dressing room at the end, he did not remember a thing about it. All he knew was that he had wanted to do his best for "the boys" who had been through so much. It was a sense of service that sustained and inspired him. They had served their country and he did not want to let them down with a bad performance. But he did not do it. It did him.

An insecure leader will feel a need to claim the credit for the victory, to be seen as the superhero who "made" it happen. The more secure we are, and the less driven by ego, the more we will surrender credit to others, to the universe, to destiny or whatever else makes sense to us.

Mahatma Ghandi made a similar plea for modesty after he had spearheaded the liberation of India from colonial rule. He did not wish to be seen as the saviour of his people, but simply as an ordinary man in extraordinary circumstances. He coined the notion of "trusteeship", that he was holding something on behalf of others, but that it was not about *him*.

It is part of human nature to sometimes want to be seen as big or special, but if we strut around after an Agincourt, claiming is was all due to us, we will be in trouble the next time we have to inspire the troops.

On a practical level, appropriate modesty can protect a leader from the inflation that often attends success, the inflation that elevates the leader to an unrealistic level from which they can apparently do no wrong, only to give others an excuse to complain the next time there is no miraculous result.

> Two young Creative Directors from a large advertising company recently went through this. They had come up with a multi-award winning campaign that had been toasted and recognized around the world. Everyone hailed them as geniuses, but they had been unable to come up with another idea for the next two years. The pressure to match the "great" piece of work had shut down the free-flowing, spontaneous nature of their creative impulse. The credit was too much; it did more damage than it was worth.

Once we get the sense that we are serving something beyond us, we – like Henry – can avoid personal aggrandisement on the back of our successes. If we can be brave enough to get out of the way, we may just make that which *could* happen into a reality. As DH Lawrence wrote in this excerpt from his poem *Song of a Man Who has come Through:*

Not I, not I, but the wind that blows through me!
A fine wind is blowing the new direction of Time.
If only I let it bear me, carry me, if only it carry me!...

If only I am keen and hard like the sheer tip of a wedge
Driven by invisible blows,
The rock will split, we shall come at the wonder, we shall find the Hesperides...

What is the knocking?
What is the knocking at the door in the night?
It is somebody wants to do us harm.

No, no, it is the three strange angels.
Admit them, admit them.

Henry has proved himself capable of admitting the "three strange angels". He would not dream of taking the credit for the "wonder" of this victory. However we might choose to think of these "angels" – the muse of fire, the spirit of the time, an unusual energy or a lucky streak – appropriate modesty may protect us from losing touch with them.

Act 5

Turning the battlefield into a garden

Photo: John Tramper

Left to right: Princess Katherine (Toby Cockerell), Queen Isabel of
France (Christian Camargo), Henry V (Mark Rylance).

Henry is encouraged to make peace and turn the battlefield into a garden. He attempts to court Princess Katherine, but realizes he has much to learn about building relationships before the political necessity becomes a heartfelt reality.

BURGUNDY   *What impediment (is) there... that... peace,*
            Should not in this best garden of the world,
            Our fertile France, put up her lovely visage?...

HENRY   *Now beshrew my father's ambition! He was thinking of civil*
            wars when he got me; therefore was I created with a
            stubborn outside, with an aspect of iron, that when I
            come to woo ladies I fright them...

QUEEN   *God, the best maker of all marriages,*
            Combine your hearts in one, your realms in one...
            That English may as French, French Englishmen,
            Receive each other, God speak this "Amen".

ACT 5 • Chorus

Towards peace

THE STORY

CHORUS   *Now we bear the King*
                Toward Calais. Grant him there; there seen,
                Heave him away upon your wingèd thoughts
                Athwart the sea... So let him land,
                And solemnly see him set on to London...
                Where that his lords desire him to have borne
                His bruisèd helmet and his bended sword
                Before him through the city; he forbids it...
                Now in London place him;
                As yet the lamentation of the French
                Invites the King of England's stay at home.
                (Until) The Emperor's coming in behalf of France,
                To order peace between them... Omit
                All the occurrences, whatever chanced,
                Till Harry's back-return again to France.

COMMENT

Far from the expectation provided at the beginning of the first four Acts, this Chorus provides a news report. We hear that Henry arrives in Calais, then England, where he is given a hero's welcome, then to London where he is given a procession, in which he refuses to carry his dented battle helmet: "Being free from vainness and self-glorious pride". After a brief respite, during which occasional raiding parties from both sides aggressed the other, the Holy Roman Emperor intervenes and attempts to broker peace between the nations.

Henry has bided his time, not able to push on for total victory but patient in the knowledge that he has made his point. The French, via the

Emperor, request a peace treaty. Henry is on his way back to France, this time on a mission for peace.

ACT 5 • Scene 1

Digesting symbols

THE STORY

Llewellyn is looking for Pistol, accompanied by Gower. The day before, on St David's day, while Llewellyn proudly wore a leek in his cap in procession, Pistol had approached him with salt, pepper and bread and bid him eat his leek. Llewellyn had done nothing to disrupt the ceremony, but swore to wear his leek until he meets Pistol again. Pistol now enters and, after a few brief meetings between Llewellyn's cudgel and his head (amidst much threatening and profanity), he is forced to eat the leek, skin and all.

Left alone Pistol contemplates his future:

> *Doth Fortune play the hussy with me now?*
> *News have I that my Nell is dead*
> *I' th' spital of a malady of France,*
> *And there my rendezvous is quite cut off.*
> *Old I do wax, and from my weary limbs*
> *Honour is cudgelled. Well, bawd I'll turn,*
> *And something lean to cutpurse of quick hand.*
> *To England will I steal, and there I'll steal,*
> *And patches will I get unto these cudgelled scars,*
> *And swear I got them in the Gallia wars.*

COMMENT

Here we see Llewellyn has learned his lesson from Henry (and we also get a subtle lesson from Shakespeare about symbols).

Henry has tried to free the Welsh captain from superficial, rule bound judgements. Now Llewellyn looks below the surface. He does not try to educate Pistol on the meaning of the symbol of the leek for the Welsh; he treats him as the scoundrel he is. He does not attempt to have him arrested for some wrong-doing – he simply makes him eat his leek. He has seen through the surface bravado to the real Pistol.

In a similar vein, symbols enable us to look beyond the surface to apprehend deeper truths. Most symbols can be viewed superficially, or we can digest them until their real meaning becomes clear. The only way some people, however, will ever digest a symbol is to eat it!

The object in dispute, the leek, is itself a symbol of this. The leek, like the onion, is multi-layered. It can be taken for just what it is – a vegetable – for what it represents historically – bravery in a garden of leeks (for the Welsh) – and for what it represents metaphorically – a symbol of purification, of having to strip away layers of meaning to get down to truth.

At the level of the appetites, food is food, the leek is not there to be understood, only to be eaten, which is why Pistol mocks Llewellyn for using it symbolically (ie taking it to a level he does not comprehend) and bids him use it physically (ie eat it). Pistol gets his comeuppance because Llewellyn has learnt to treat each individual according to his deserts – and Pistol deserves to have his mockery rebound on him. If he can't be made to eat his words, he can be made to do what he teased Llewellyn about, and eat the leek.

Pistol remains unrepentant and irredeemable. The death of friends, the death of his wife from the pox, cudgelled honour; nothing can turn him away from a life of crime and the sating of appetite. Having lost all he will now turn his latest beating into an opportunity to beg, and gull fools into parting with their money.

Shakespeare knows there will always be Pistols around and does not write a morality play where they reform. We need to be able to recognize them, not to get taken in as Llewellyn was at first. Henry may even need some of these "dogs of war" to supplement the more honourable foot soldiers, like Williams. But he does not mix with them as a leader, and he disciplines them ruthlessly when they are caught in their corruption.

By drawing attention to a symbol in this scene Shakespeare is, I believe, warning his audience that there will be more symbolic resonance in the scene to come. The resolution of Henry's journey is not to be seen merely on a physical-historical level, but allegorically too.

ACT 5 • Scene 2

Turning the battlefield into a garden

THE STORY

The two Courts of England and France finally meet for a peace negotiation. Henry, Exeter and other lords, King Charles of France, Queen Isabel, the Duke of Burgundy and other French, among them Princess Katherine and Alice. The Duke of Burgundy, who has instigated the meeting, addresses both kings:

> *What impediment (is) there... that... peace,*
> *Should not in this best garden of the world,*
> *Our fertile France, put up her lovely visage?*
> *Alas, she hath from France too long been chased...*
> *And as all our vineyards, fallows, meads, and hedges,*
> *Defective in their natures, grow to wildness,*
> *Even so our houses and ourselves and children*
> *Have lost, or do not learn for want of time,*
> *The sciences that should become our country,*
> *But grow like savages—as soldiers will*
> *That nothing do but meditate on blood—*
> *To swearing and stern looks, diffused attire,*
> *And everything that seems unnatural.*

Henry replies that peace will follow if his demands in the prepared treaty are met. The others go off to consider the proposals in full, leaving Henry alone with Katherine (who is one of Henry's "capital demands" in the treaty) and her chaperone Alice. We find that Katherine's English lessons have not yet paid off, but Henry is grateful, thinking this will save him from elaborate wooing:

HENRY *I am glad thou canst speak no better English, for if thou*
couldst, thou wouldst find me... a plain King. I know no
ways to mince it in love, but directly to say, "I love you";
then if you urge me farther... I wear out my suit...
If I could win a lady... by vaulting into my saddle
with my armour on my back, I should quickly leap into a wife...
KATHERINE *Is it possible dat I sould love de ennemi of*
France?
HENRY *No, it is not possible you should love the*
enemy of France, Kate. But in loving me, you should
love the friend of France, for I love France so well that
I will not part with a village of it, I will have it all
mine; and Kate, when France is mine, and I am yours,
then yours is France, and you are mine.
KATHERINE *I cannot tell vat is dat.*

Henry tries to tell her in French, which is only slightly worse than her English. He then returns to his own language: "But Kate, dost thou understand thus much English? Canst thou love me?" She replies:

I cannot tell.
HENRY *Now beshrew my father's ambition! He was thinking of civil*
wars when he got me; therefore was I created with a
stubborn outside, with an aspect of iron, that when I
come to woo ladies I fright them. Put off your maiden
blushes, take me by the hand and say,
"Harry of England, I am thine"— (and) I will tell thee
aloud, "England is thine, Ireland is thine, France is

thine, and Henry Plantagenet is thine… Therefore, queen of all,
Katherine, break thy mind to me in broken English:
wilt thou have me?

KATHERINE *Dat is as it shall please le roi mon père.*

HENRY *Nay, it will please him well, Kate…*

KATHERINE *Den it sall also content me.*

Henry kisses her as the lords re-enter. Burgundy inquires how Henry has got on with the Princess:

HENRY *I cannot so conjure up the spirit of love in her*
that he will appear in his true likeness.

BURGUNDY *If you would conjure in her, you must make a circle… (and)*
teach her to know my meaning; for maids well summered
and warm kept are like flies at Bartholomew-tide… and then
they will endure handling which before would not abide looking on.

HENRY *This moral ties me over to time, and a hot summer: and so*
I shall catch the fly, your cousin, in the latter end.

Henry agrees to be patient. The treaty has been ratified and is sealed when King Charles agrees to the marriage. The Queen adds her blessing:

QUEEN ISABEL *God, the best maker of all marriages,*
Combine your hearts in one, your realms in one.
That never may ill office or fell jealousy,
Thrust in between the paction of these kingdoms
To make divorce of their incorporate league;
That English may as French, French Englishmen,
Receive each other, God speak this "Amen".

FROM BATTLEFIELD TO GARDEN

And thus the play ends, far from the cries of the battlefield, in a peace negotiation and a courtship. The style changes from military heroic to romantic comedy. The leadership questions posed by this Act centre on how to turn a battlefield into a garden, and how to turn a Warrior into a keeper of the peace.

These themes bring us closer to the characters of the Great Mother and the Medicine Woman. There is a move away from *doing* to *being*, from task to relationship, from issue to image.

In the mode of the Medicine Woman I will be attempting to imagine new roles and desirable futures that do not yet exist. In drawing on the Great Mother I will attempt to focus on relationships and look at the bigger picture with the eyes of nurture and sustainability. There will be fewer practical examples and more calls to the imagination. You are invited to suspend your disbelief and allow the images to work in their own peculiar way. In *King Lear* a blind man is asked how he sees the world; he replies "I see it feelingly". It is a good way of seeing our last scene, "feelingly".

As Burgundy points out, if both kings just keep doing what they are used to doing – fighting – there may be nothing left to fight for. France, "the best garden of the world", will go to rack and ruin:

> And as all our vineyards, fallows, meads, and hedges,
> Defective in their natures, grow to wildness,
> Even so our houses and ourselves and children...
>   grow like savages—as soldiers will
> That nothing do but meditate on blood.

Some organizations are so obsessed with preparing for battle – and de-layering to get fighting fit – that they lose their best people. They get so lean that no one wants to work there anymore. When I coach the people who have left they do not lack ambition, drive or skill, but they are looking for a place that welcomes human beings. The Warriors will get results but they will be unlikely to make work enjoyable. In today's climate, to keep good people you need to create a culture that develops their potential and nurture an atmosphere that they will want to be part of, day after day, year after year.

While the excitement of the struggle will keep people engaged, for a while, it is not sustainable. It leads to burn out, as it did for so many in the so-called yuppie boom of the 80's. If we only "meditate on blood" eventually we start to see any garden we come across as simply a watering hole en route to the next battle, rather than see the garden as something innately valuable, and as important in the long run as the battlefield.

Too much focus on the battle leads to stress-related illness for individuals, but the effects do not stop there. They spread to the community (where many currently experience alienation and exclusion) and to the planet itself, which needs to be treated more like a garden and less like a stockroom to be plundered at will. A director from the Environment Agency identified the current shareholder biased, short-term thinking as being indirectly responsible for more environmental damage that the nuclear disaster at Chernobyl. People are increasingly paid to focus on the short-term victory at the expense of long-term sustainability. As he said: "When I ask people if they want their grandchildren to enjoy the same quality of life as they do, they say 'Of course!', but most of the organizations they work for, as corporate entities, are not even beginning to do what needs to be done to make that wish a reality."

Sir Peter Parker, former Chairman of the British Rail Board, once said:

I believe that an outspoken commitment to environmental policy and practice – defined and public and transparent – is expected of any competitive and ambitious company... More and more business leaders of pace-making enterprises have come to see it as central to good business and its corporate citizenship – for all sorts of reasons, including commercial self-interest and genuine conviction.

Our Business civilisation has got too used to its bad habits, infecting land, sea and air, scything forests, raining acid on ourselves, drilling holes in the sky, threatening bio-diversity... We are being warned, the global market system needs to be saved from itself and its universal appetite, and this is not only a matter for global governance summits or boardrooms, it is a matter for communities and the individual. The environmental fight is too important to be left to the generals.

(Royal Society of Arts Lecture; reported in *The Independent*, 5 January 2001)

It is as individuals that we must change first. How we then go about creating that same opportunity for change in our people is another question...

FROM SIEGE TO PEACE

We encountered another version of this dilemma at the Globe Theatre after the opening season. The project had been fighting to survive for 25 years, always against the odds, always defending itself against attack. Inevitably, a "head down", siege mentality had developed. Suddenly the battle was won; a beautiful new/old theatre was there, up and running. The siege mentality was no longer necessary, what was required now was the ability to tend the garden and fill the building with "flowering" performance. The shift was too hard for some of the original fighting pioneers to make. They knew their strength was in the battle, others' strengths would be nurturing the territory that the battle had achieved, and the best thing for them was to leave, and find another battle.

This is one way out. There are, undoubtedly, some leaders who excel in surviving a siege, and others who blossom in a peaceful boom. (Churchill, in recent history, was the former, Bill Clinton, arguably, the latter.) There are others, however, who can do both. Nelson Mandela notably survived a 27-year "siege" in a prison cell, and then taught others how to put down the gun. Here is a piece he quoted after his release (which was adapted from American writer Marianne Williamson):

Our deepest fear is not that we are inadequate.
Our deepest fear is that we are powerful beyond measure.
It is our light, not our darkness, that most frightens us.
We ask ourselves, who am I to be brilliant, gorgeous, talented and fabulous?
Actually, who are you NOT to be? You are a child of God.
Your playing small doesn't serve the world.
There's nothing enlightened about shrinking so that other people
Won't feel insecure around you.
We were born to make manifest the glory
that is within us.
It's not just in some of us; it's in EVERYONE!

*And as we let our own light shine, we unconsciously give other people
permission to do the same.*
As we are liberated from our fear, our presence automatically liberates others!

It is this ability to believe in the potential of others, and to liberate that
potential, that signifies the true "gardener-leader" at work. These words
do not inspire us to defeat others, but to "grow" them, to share our
knowledge in the service of a greater good. If we do this it becomes self-
perpetuating. The idea of giving others "permission" to do the same is
important too. As the mythologist Michael Meade says: "There is no
mission without permission". If we find a mission that enables us to shine
and make a difference, others will automatically want to follow suit. We
must show the way and lead by example if we are to nurture a thriving
garden.

INTO THE GARDEN – CHANGING THE METAPHOR

Changing the metaphor changes the energy. Most people think they are
afraid of failure; Nelson Mandela conjures images of dark and light, and
many see they may just be afraid of making a real difference; in other
words, afraid of success. When individuals make a real change I often
find that there is a shift in imagery in their inner world too. The dreams
they have, the pictures or movies they are drawn too, contain different
images and themes than those that sustained them in their old character
structure. If we then wish to share the possibility of change with others
we will need to change the metaphors we use to talk to others about
work. We cannot begin effectively to change the culture of an organization
without also changing its imagery, and therefore changing the "story" the
organization tells about itself.

Metaphors are powerful; they carry meaning and can change the way
we think about things. As James Autry writes in his book *Love and Profit
– The Art of Caring Leadership*:

By invoking the metaphor of sports teams these days, we imply that... there
must be winners and losers, stars who play and benchwarmers who watch,

194

that our personal success is measured only by numbers on the scoreboard and not by how well we played, and that our value to society is transitory, at best...

By invoking the metaphor of community, we imply that we in business are bound by a fellowship of endeavour in which we commit to mutual goals, in which each contribution is recognized and credited... in which our success contributes to the success of others... in which we are free to express what we feel as well as what we think, in which our value to society is directly related to the quality of our commitment and effort, and in which we take care of one another.

All this is high sounding, to be sure, *but we intend metaphors as inspiration to make things as they are not now but should be...* Perhaps team works well for your enterprise... now. The time will come, sooner or later, when your team players will realize that winning always comes at the end of the game, but there is no end to the work. At that point, work looks a lot more like life – a process that requires us to make the most of it every day and to concentrate on the journey, not the destination.

When your team reaches that point, you'll need another metaphor. Be prepared.

From sports team to community, from battlefield to garden, the metaphorical images we draw from at work help define the reality. Part of what we do in the world can always be defined as a struggle, of one sort or another, and we usually have plenty of images around to help us evoke the energy needed to survive that struggle. A wise leader will make sure that the struggle is not the only energy with metaphorical support. They will take care to imagine another part of work that can be more nurturing and sustainable, even enjoyable.

There are many martial images in our story, but Shakespeare ends with peace and marriage, not war and struggle. We should not ignore this message. Some CEO's distrust this scene – "Surely at work there is no respite; you may win a battle but you never win the war, if you ever leave the battlefield you will become complacent" – the inference being that they will get to the garden when they retire.

But internally, metaphorically and psychologically, when you retire it is too late. If the garden has not been nurtured carefully over many years, it will not be a garden but a jungle or a wasteland. If we simply "meditate on blood" or success or shareholder value we may end up like the Spanish poet Antonio Machado:

THE WIND, ONE BRILLIANT DAY...

The wind, one brilliant day, called to my soul with an odour of jasmine.

"In return for the odour of my jasmine, I'd like all the odour of your roses."

"I have no roses; all the flowers in my garden are dead."

"Well then, I'll take the withered petals
and the yellow leaves and the waters of the fountain."

The wind left. And I wept. And I said to myself.

"What have you done with the garden that was entrusted to you?"

(Translated by Robert Bly)

For me, looking after the garden does not mean giving up the struggle, but making sure we know how to restore ourselves (and others) in-between the times of struggle. The flowers of learning and relationship that Burgundy argues need protection can wither and die if we do not water them inside us. This means paying attention to them, developing our "garden" as consciously as we might develop a career, and finding an appropriate balance between going out into the world and exploring the world within. In medieval times the gardens were walled, and were the only outdoor environments in which gentlemen would take off their swords. We need to create those environments consciously throughout our working lives.

As work plays an increasingly important part in people's lives, and as business plays an increasingly influential role in the world at large, I believe that leaders of the future will be called on to play this new role of "gardener-leader". They will need to be more aware of the equal importance of the battle and the garden. This is what Henry struggles to learn from Katherine and Burgundy in our scene.

TAKING OFF THE ARMOUR

A leader will always inform the culture of their organization, consciously or unconsciously. So if, as a culture, England finds it hard to stop fighting, we must look to Henry:

> *If I could win a lady... by vaulting into my saddle*
> *with my armour on my back, I should quickly leap into a wife...*
> *Now beshrew my father's ambition! He was thinking of civil*
> *wars when he got me; therefore was I created with a*
> *stubborn outside, with an aspect of iron, that when I*
> *come to woo ladies I fright them.*

He does not yet know how to take the armour off. As the young Prince Hal he spent his time in taverns and in castles fighting rebels. As Henry V he has prepared for and engaged in battle. He is so much more used to fighting than building a relationship that he can't help treating the Princess as if she were a town to be besieged until she surrenders, like Harfleur. But (also like Harfleur) this victory will take him longer than expected.

Henry cannot get Katherine to say she loves him, only that she will agree to the political expediency of the marriage, to please her father. Henry admits to Burgundy: "I cannot so conjure up the spirit of love in her that he will appear in his true likeness." Burgundy, as the peacemaker, attempts to teach Henry a lesson in relationships. He says, rather elliptically, that Henry must "make (conjure) a circle" and, more practically, that he must learn patience and allow the courtship to grow over the length of a whole summer, rather than be sealed immediately.

THE UNION OF OPPOSITES

This scene is the first and only time we see three women on the stage, and it is no accident that they are a Maiden (Princess Katherine), a Mother (Queen Isabel) and a Crone (the old waiting woman, Alice). These three are symbols of the Feminine principle, the triple-fold goddess of mythology. It is a sign that we are moving away from the masculine principles of logic, law and forcefulness and into emotion, intuition and surrender.

A circle is also a feminine image, representing the primordial womb and the creative void; it symbolizes unity, wholeness and completeness in all cultures. The Globe itself, with its "wooden O" that the first Chorus introduces us to, is designed to be inclusive in exactly this way. When Henry complains to Burgundy that Katherine does not love him, Burgundy replies: "If you would conjure (the spirit of love) in her, you must make a circle." Henry is not used to circles, his life has been ruled by lines and squares. This "circle" that has to be "conjured" is a magic circle – it evokes invisible forces, not those that can be measured. The circle will require Henry, who has done such visible and forceful outward work, to go inside and work with invisible worlds, in order to earn a lasting relationship.

He wishes the Princess to love him because he seeks a true marriage, not a hollow political engagement. Symbolically, a marriage is a union of opposites, the coming together of that which had seemed separate and apart. The warring blunt English King and the carefree romantic French Princess become symbols of all that can seem different and opposed in life: man and woman, masculine and feminine, light and dark, sun and moon, war and peace, winning and losing, profit and love, work and family, above and below, spirit and matter, conscious and unconscious. All of us can learn from these mighty pairs of opposites. Just as we can always learn from that which we see as different or opposite to us (which is why those who open their eyes to it find such value in diversity within their workforce). The circle which Henry is advised to "conjure" is the place that can contain the opposites. It is here we can connect with and integrate the learning we are offered by the "other" or opposite.

Burgundy, in essence, suggests that Henry take off his armour and give up the need for a quick victory, that he learn the way of the circle and the nature of nurture. For most of us, giving up old ways of being is extremely difficult. We risk moving from unconscious competence to conscious incompetence. Henry's risk would be to appear without his "aspect of iron", his armour, and be seen as a vulnerable human being. It is a frightening prospect, with a worthwhile goal. As that famous writer Anonymous once said:

RISK

To laugh is to risk appearing the fool.
To weep is to risk appearing sentimental.
To reach out for another is to risk involvement.
To expose feeling is to risk exposing your true self.
To place your ideas, your dreams, before the crowd is to risk their loss.
To love is to risk not being loved in return.
To live is to risk dying.
To hope is to risk failure.
But the risk must be taken, because the greatest hazard in life is to risk nothing.

People may avoid suffering and sorrow, but they simply cannot learn, feel, change, grow, love, live.
Chained by certitudes, they are slaves, they have forfeited freedom.
Only a person who risks... is free.

Ultimately, I believe, we all seek this kind of freedom. It is most naturally accessible to the Medicine Woman character, the archetype that Katherine embodies, and which Henry wishes to woo. "This moral ties me over to time, and a hot summer". He agrees to learn a new way and to take his armour off to enter the garden.

CONJURING A CIRCLE

These themes are elusive and hard to pin down. As a leader I believe I experienced them in directing Act 5 Scene 2 in the rehearsal room.

We were an all-male cast and had soldiered manfully through the play with lots of ideas, focus and direction. But we always seemed to run out of time for this last, crucial scene. Whenever we did come to it we got stuck in difficult arguments. There may have been peace at the end of the story, but there certainly wasn't peace at the end of our rehearsals for Act 5. We kept putting off any resolution until the opening night loomed into view. We now allocated lots of time and approached the scene very diligently as a *problem* to be solved. We tried it every which way. No good.

Finally it occurred to me to try the mythodramatic approach that we had been developing. This involved evoking the energies within scenes and sharing physical experiences of the themes. We had done this for the masculine energies in the play at the old airfield, building fires and jumping through them to get a taste of the siege in Act 3. It felt like we needed to try the equivalent for the feminine energies in Act 5. The cast collectively agreed to take a risk; to let go of any ideas about the scene and simply create a space in which we could explore its innate energy.

At the next rehearsal the actors showed up with any objects, poems, food or anything else they associated with images and themes in the scene. We created a huge circle in the middle of the floor, and decorated it with flowers and cloth. We entered the circle with cushions, blankets, candles and other objects, and waited. We had no plans – or perhaps the only plan was to give up control; to attempt what we felt Henry was being asked to do at this stage of the play. To give up the known, to accept that that which had got him this far could get him no further. To conjure a circle and see if something of love, courtship, patience, summer and fruitfulness would emerge.

Inevitably there were a few moments of embarrassed silence – and then, suddenly, as if by magic, something else began to flow. Someone spoke of a lover who had died; another spoke of falling in love for the first time. Another of fear of commitment. Another read a poem expressing his terror of vulnerability. On and on, the actors spoke spontaneously of their personal experience of the energies and themes that had eluded our intellectual pursuit of them in previous rehearsals. We ended up singing a song and sharing a loaf of bread from a Swedish wedding. It was, without doubt, the strangest afternoon I have ever spent in a rehearsal room, and in the end, will probably prove to be one of the most effective.

The next time we got to this scene there was nothing physically different in the staging, but emotionally there was another energy present. And there was no more conflict. It was as if, collectively, we had risked taking off our armour and somehow our playing of the scene had transformed. Our shared understanding of each other's experiences of love and sacrifice and difficulty seemed to infuse the words with new meaning. Suddenly, by giving up, by getting out of our siege mentality towards the scene, by conjuring a circle, magic had happened. As a group of men, we had surrendered to the feminine; to the unconscious forces that Burgundy alludes to, and courted the right to hold this energy to end our play.

COURTING THE INNER MARRIAGE

So what the hell might all this mean to us as leaders?

I know it would not have worked for me if I had been the only one to give up ideas and control. In that rehearsal I needed enough of the team behind me to be able collectively to take a risk. Without mutual trust it would not have happened. It was also important that we had a structure we could return too, we did not throw away what we had, we held it in reserve while we experimented with other options. And we were willing to learn about each other as human beings, rather than study our functions like cogs in a machine. We were willing to risk a change of approach and embrace our less familiar characters.

Most leaders I meet acknowledge that the old ways don't work any more, that if they don't adapt to change they will wither, if not die, and that the future appears even more unpredictable now than a generation ago. Ongoing development is no longer an option, it is essential.

Most effective leaders have little or nothing to learn from their own well-rehearsed style, or favourite character. We know them well, we play them well, and we get paid well to do so. Not much to develop there. *But*, in the least favourite character – in the one we ignore if we can, and may only pay lip service to when we can't – there lies our potential. Like Henry, it may well be that we have played our favourite character to its limit. That which has got us so far can get us no further.

Henry has proved himself as the victorious Warrior and the successful King, and even though he has visited the feminine roles (to vision the future and survive the "dark night") he is certainly not as comfortable there as in the masculine. Now his challenge changes dramatically.

When we first meet Princess Katherine she is learning a new language, interested in change and transformation. Her marriage will bring healing to the wounded garden of France and allow a new cycle of creative life to flow. She knows how to play the dynamic feminine Medicine Woman, and it is she Henry wishes to court.

In psychology we would say that Henry is also courting the inner feminine. By courting the Medicine Woman without he also seeks the Medicine Woman within. He is prepared to stretch and learn. As the German poet Rainer Maria Rilke puts it:

> *Take your well disciplined strengths*
> *and stretch them between two*
> *opposing poles. Because inside human beings*
> *is where God learns.*

> (From *Just as the Winged Energy of Delight,* translated by Robert Bly)

If Henry is successful in this endeavour he will become a more complete leader. He will learn how to plant the seeds in his new and extended territory and nurture them.

One of the most practical ways to court the least favourite character is to engage in an activity related to it. We can court the Warrior through determined and energetic activity, the Good King through order and structure, the Medicine Woman through spontaneity and creativity, and the Great Mother through relaxation and nurture.

We often ask people who wish to extend their learning beyond the seminar to choose an activity related to the character they feel they most need to learn to play as a leader, and commit to it for a reasonable amount of time.

I did this a few years ago. I realized that I was limiting my potential because I had no access to the Warrior. I was nice and polite but not forceful or assertive. I took up karate for a year. I learnt to defend myself and to aggress others in a safe and disciplined environment. I probably wouldn't do it again, and I will certainly never go out to pick a fight, but this activity brought the character of the Warrior closer. I am much more able to hold my ground and stand up for what I believe, especially in public, than I ever was before.

Activities To Practise Potentials

STATIC MASCULINE	*DYNAMIC MASCULINE*
Action planning	Competitive sports
Time management	Working out – gym
Strategy games – chess/bridge	Martial arts – karate
Reading (non-fiction)	Punch bag
Reviewing	Physical tasks/targets
Gathering information	Extreme sports
Clearing clutter	Archery/Shooting
Ordering/tidying up	Hunting/Fishing
Organizing wardrobe/desk	Mountaineering
Serious classical music (Bach)	Rock music
STATIC FEMININE	**DYNAMIC FEMININE**
Relaxation	Artistic: Painting
Walk in nature	Dance class
Being in or near water	Singing
Slow hot bath	Poetry
Proper diet	Pottery
Meditation	Amateur dramatics
Gardening	Playing/Self expression
Massage – aromatherapy	Spontaneity
Tai Chi/Yoga	Doing the unfamiliar
Quiet time with family	Brainstorming
Music: slow, choral, chanting	Jazz music

Just as an actor needs to practise and rehearse playing a character before they (and the audience) can fully believe in it, so we need to rehearse new leadership roles before we and others believe in it. If we try it too soon at work we hear the dreaded words; "Ooh, look who's been on a course then!" We advise people to practise the activity related to the character outside of work first. As you become used to it, it will naturally begin to become available to you, wherever you are.

The activities invoke the energy of the character. We rehearse playing the character by engaging in the activity. The more we rehearse the closer the character comes. Eventually the new character begins to change our assumptions about ourselves. Instead of going around with the internal impression "You can't really stand up for yourself, you'd never be any

203

good in a fight", I learned a new message, "You can stand up for yourself and defend yourself when necessary. Sometimes you even enjoy it!" Having experienced this in the karate classes for a year, externally, it became part of my nature, internally. I had learned to play a new character, which from then on would always be a part of my repertoire.

A small word of warning. As human beings we have a tendency to take our favourite character with us into situations that call for our least favourite character.

> I was once coaching a very ambitious and upwardly mobile investment banker, who strongly identified with the Warrior but recognized that he had most to learn from the static feminine Great Mother. However, on reading the above lists, he felt he was already engaging in most of the suggested activities. When asked if he ever had a massage he replied: "Yes, every week, except the masseur is too gentle, I have to keep telling him to dig deep and work the muscles harder." We asked him if he ever went for a walk in nature; "Oh yes, I go hawking every weekend." I gave it one more try: "Well, do you ever just hang out by large bodies of water?" Without a flicker of hesitation he came straight back; "Oh yes, I do that as well, every summer I go shark fishing."

If we wish to court a new character we need to be open to what that character has to offer, or we will end up imposing our old habits on the new "relationship". If, like Henry, we give time to this courtship we will earn the "inner marriage" of old and new characters. As the Queen says:

> *Combine your hearts in one, your realms in one...*
> *That English may as French, French Englishmen,*
> *Receive each other.*

We can combine the "England" we manage already with the "France" we wish to court. This new relationship can end old struggles and open up the prospect of a fruitful future in our newly extended territory.

EPILOGUE

Achieving the garden

THE STORY

CHORUS *Thus far with rough and all-unable pen*
Our bending author hath pursued the story,
In little room confining mighty men,
Mangling by starts the full course of their glory.
Small time, but in that small most greatly lived
This star of England. Fortune made his sword,
By which the world's best garden he achieved,
And of it left his son imperial lord.
Henry the Sixth, in infant bands crowned King
Of France and England, did this King succeed,
Whose state so many had the managing
That they lost France and made his England bleed,
Which oft our stage hath shown—and, for their sake,
In your fair minds let this acceptance take.

MAKING THE DIFFERENCE YOU CAN MAKE

Henry achieved the "world's best garden" but only ruled it for a "small time". His infant son became prey to political manipulations that led to the Wars of the Roses. The country had to survive the tyranny of Richard III and the confusion of a change of religion under Henry VIII before harmony was restored under Elizabeth I, who presided over the English Renaissance, Shakespeare and the original Globe Theatre. If history teaches us anything, it is that no achievement lasts forever: "Small time, but in that small most greatly lived this star of England".

We cannot know what the implications of our actions will be long term, or if we will make a lasting difference, but what we can do is live our lives as "greatly" as possible. Not necessarily "great" in the roll of history or media headlines, but "great" as in doing our best to make the world a better place.

The world of work will keep changing, the strategic skills required to be a successful leader will undoubtedly change from time to time, but the human nature of inspirational leadership will stay essentially the same, as I hope this journey through a 400-year-old play has proved.

If we know what inspires us to get up in the morning, if we feel we are in the service of something greater than ourselves, and if we can pass that on to others in an appropriate way, we will inspire them.

If I am to do this I need to be able to bring all of myself to the table, into the office, into the training room or boardroom. I couldn't even attempt it if I felt I had to hide bits of me away, bury them deep inside or leave them in the car park. Life is to be lived, as someone wise once said: "It is important that when death finds you, it finds you alive." Working life is to be lived too. In my experience, there are far too many people who "die" at work, who become less than they could be, who get reduced from their potential as a human *being* to a human *doing*, fulfilling some corporate function and waiting for 5pm, 6pm or whenever, just to get home. People who end up living for evenings, weekends, holidays or retirement, because they are unable fully to inhabit their working days.

There are times when I have done this. I hope I will never do it again. If I succeed in this aim it will be because of the leaders, mentors, coaches, poets, playwrights and other great thinkers and friends who have inspired me. If we have been inspired to make a difference ourselves, it is not an effort to try and inspire others, it is a joy. To do the bit that we can do. To make the difference that only we can make.

I WILL NOT DIE AN UNLIVED LIFE

I will not die an unlived life.
I will not live in fear of falling
or catching fire.
I choose to inhabit my days,
to allow my living to open me
to make me less afraid,
more accessible,

to loosen my heart
until it becomes a wing,
a torch, a promise.
I choose to risk my significance;
To live
so that which came to me as seed
goes to the next as blossom
and that which came to me
as blossom
goes on as fruit.

(From *I Will Not Die an Unlived Life* by Dawna Markova)

That is achieving the garden.

Bibliography

Autry, James. *Love and Profit*. Avon Books, 1991.

Bly, Robert (Editors James Hillman and Michael Meade). *The Rag and Bone Shop of the Heart*. Harper Perrenial, 1993.

Chetwynd, Tom. *A Dictionary of Symbols*. Harper Collins, 1982.

Cook, Liz and Rothwell, Brian. *The X and Y of Leadership*. The Industrial Society, 2000.

Cox, Murray. *Shakespeare as Prompter*. Jessica Kingsley Publishers, 1994.

Dawkins, Peter. *The Pattern of Initiation*. The Francis Bacon Research Trust, 1981.

Emunah, Renee. *Acting for Real*. Brunner/Mazal, 1994.

Gardner, Brian. *Up the Line to Death*. Methuen & Co Ltd, 1964.

Goleman, Daniel. *Working with Emotional Intelligence*. Bloomsbury, 1999.

Greenleaf, Robert. *The Servant as a Leader*. The Robert K Greenleaf Center, Indianapolis, 1991.

Gurr, Andrew. *King Henry V*. Cambridge University Press, 1992.

Handy, Charles. *The Search for Meaning*. Lemos & Crane, 1996.

Handy, Charles. *Gods of Management*. Century, 1978.

Hibert, Christopher. *Agincourt*. BT Batsford Ltd, 1964.

Hill, Gareth. *Masculine and Feminine*. Shambahala, 1992.

Hillman, James. *The Soul's Code*. Bantam Books, 1997.

Jaworski, Joseph. *Synchronicity*. Berrett-Koehler, 1998.

Moore, Robert. *King, Warrior, Magician, Lover*. HarperSanFrancisco, 1990.

Nair, Keshavan. *A Higher Standard of Leadership*. Berrett-Koehler, 1997.

Pine, Joseph. *The Experience Economy*. Harvard Business School Press, 1999.

Pogson, Beryl. *In the East my Pleasure Lies*. Quacks Books Ltd, 1994.

Ridley, M. *The New Temple Shakespeare, King Henry IV, First Part*. JM Dent & Sons Ltd, 1934.

Ridley, M. *The New Temple Shakespeare, King Henry IV, Second Part*. JM Dent & Sons Ltd, 1934.

Schuthzman, Mandy. *Playing Boal*. Routledge, 1994.

Turner, David. *Liberating Leadership*. The Industrial Society, 1998.

Verma, Rajiva. *Myth, Ritual and Shakespeare.* Spantech Publishers PVT Ltd, 1990.

Whyte, David. *The Heart Aroused.* Doubleday, 1994.

Whyte, David. *The House of Belonging.* Many Rivers Press, 1996.

Zohar, Danah. *Rewiring the Corporate Brain.* Berrett-Koehler, 1997.

Permissions